6-8-23

SPEAKING FROM THE HEART

SPEAKING
from the
Heart

Preaching

With

Passion

Richard F. Ward

Abingdon Press
Nashville, Tennessee

SPEAKING FROM THE HEART:
Preaching with Passion

Copyright © 1992 by Abingdon Press

This book is printed on recycled, acid-free paper.

Library of Congress Cataloging-in-Publication Data

Ward, Richard F.
    Speaking from the heart : preaching with passion / Richard F. Ward.
        p.   cm. — (Abingdon preacher's library)
    ISBN 0-687-39166-0
    1. Preaching.   I. Title.   II. Series.
    BV4211 . 2 . W29   1992   92-3671
    251—dc20   CIP

Scripture quotations are from the New Revised Standard Version of the Bible,
copyright © 1989 by the Division of Christian Education of the National Council of
the Churches of Christ in the U.S.A. Used by permission.

"no time ago" is reprinted from XAIPE by E. E. Cummings, Edited by George
James Firmage, by permission of Liveright Publishing Corporation. Copyright
1950 by E. E. Cummings. Copyright © 1979, 1978, 1973 by Nancy T. Andrews.
Copyright © 1979, 1973 by George James Firmage.

MANUFACTURED IN THE UNITED STATES OF AMERICA

*I dedicate this book to my parents,
Dalton and Marjory Ward,
for they first taught me how to speak,
to learn, and to write.*

Contents

SPEAKING FROM THE HEART

Foreword

The longest walk in the world for preachers is the journey from the pulpit back to the chancel when we sense we have failed to convey the fire of the Spirit in our hearts. Usually, it was not that the sermon outline was wrong or the theology faulty. It was, instead, the way we felt ourselves blocking the message, obstructing the energies of the Spirit which had initially mobilized our insight and urgency. It is as though the words we delivered were only the skeleton of the living, embodied truth which had filled us with passion in our study.

Richard Ward identifies with all of us who have ever made that long walk back from the pulpit to the chancel. He has himself known the experience, and he recounts what it was like in the pages that follow.

But he does more than share the vulnerability which is common to all of us who preach the gospel. He develops an historical, theological and practical understanding of how we can embody the good news that we yearn to tell to our congregations. He does this while avoiding two of the most common pitfalls in our efforts to improve sermon delivery:

1. Reducing the issue to nothing more than a matter of technique.

2. Ignoring technique all together.

Because it is easy to fall into either of these traps, it is worth looking at both of them before we begin to consider Ward's balanced approach.

The temptation to reduce preaching solely to technique is especially appealing in an age of high tech solutions. We reason that surely there must be some system that can assure our success in the pulpit, just as there are new computer programs to do everything from reorganizing our finances to diagnosing the rattle in our car to analyzing interstellar phenomena. But, in fact, method alone is never sufficient to communicate the life-transforming power of the gospel. Having listened to hundreds of preachers over the last fifteen years, I can call to mind dozens of ministers whose theology was sound, whose voices were clear and well supported, whose gestures and inflection were exemplary, and whose sermons still fell flat.

When their peers analyzed what had gone wrong, they often found themselves initially baffled. After all, everything was technically correct, including the exposition of the Scripture, selection of illustrations, articulation and the coherence of the outline. But in the last analysis there was no passion, no empathic identification with the pain of human life, no sense of the irrepressible power of the risen Christ animating the words, gestures, facial expression, and inflection of the preacher. Instead, the mechanics of public presentation, polished as they were, served to mute the vitalities of the Spirit within the preacher.

The other distortion in the delivery of sermons, equally deleterious, is a failure to employ the essential methods of clear and effective public speech and to justify that failure by appealing to absolute reliance on the Spirit. Words are mumbled, gestures constricted, and there is about the entire presentation a sense that the preacher has not taken seriously the exercise of the gifts of thought and skill which God expects all of us to use.

How then can we draw upon the best methods of public speaking without succumbing to a methodological aridity?

This is exactly the question which Richard Ward answers with grace and wisdom in the following pages. There is no simple way to summarize the development of his process, but I believe preachers, both those with years of experience and those just beginning, will find here a way of understanding the task of public proclamation that is rooted in the Bible and theology.

The title of the book, *Speaking from the Heart: Preaching with Passion,* identifies Ward's great theme and names the hope we have for our own witness to the gospel: to speak from our hearts to the hearts of our listeners. We do not mean this in some narrow privatistic sense of what we know to be true simply as individuals. But we want to speak from the "heart strangely warmed," from the core of what the Spirit has revealed and done to us as creatures of God in need of hope and healing. We have known God's restoring power in our lives, otherwise we would not be preachers; but the day to day, hour to hour pastoral demands of deaths, illnesses, family crises, budgetary problems and congregational squabbles can easily quench the Spirit's flames within us.

This book offers practical help to remove whatever obstructs the working of God in our speech and bodily expression. Ward's solutions fuse together the best principles of public speaking with historical and theological insight. The result is that the reader is not misled into either the distortion of a method without spirituality or a spirituality without method.

Ward draws on the discipline of performance studies to help us preachers claim our continuity with the early Christian preachers, and to help us acknowledge the sources of personal experience which influence us every time we stand to declare the gospel. Rather than set historical and personal approaches to preaching against each other, he builds a structure for understanding how tradition and the preacher's experience are interwoven in effective proclamation. We come to see that the appropriate use of our selves and our life experience can be a continuation of the rhetorical and homiletical strategies of the early church, particularly as manifest in the ministry of Paul the apostle.

The result of Ward's historical analysis and contemporary homiletical reflection is to give us a renewed interior confidence so that when we walk from the pulpit to the chancel, we can trust more completely that the Spirit has moved through us in ways that can reshape our listeners' lives.

To summarize his work: Ward assists preachers in finding a way to *embody* the insights of contemporary homiletical theory as living qualities in our preaching. We do not tell stories to entertain. We do not draw on personal experience to display ourselves. Rather we engage these methods as an extension of the Spirit's reaching out to the stories and experience of our listener's lives in order that they might be transformed by the saving power of God.

Thus, Ward's book, while it is filled with practical exercises and suggestions, is more than a text in homiletical method. It is a work of practical spirituality for the preacher. It is practical in its down-to-earth examples and exercises. Yet it presents a homiletical spirituality by showing how these examples and exercises continue the tradition of proclamation that began in the witness of the early church.

I hope that this book will take its place in the larger theological movement of our age which seeks to realize more completely the liberation of human beings to claim all that God has intended for their lives: compassion, justice, peace, the saving power of grace. Preachers whose delivery incarnates these qualities will proclaim the good news of Christ in ways that liberate their listeners.

As preachers appropriate Ward's insights into their own delivery they will find themselves lifted up as they walk back from the pulpit to the chancel. For they will sense that by speaking from the heart, that by preaching with passion, they have helped their congregation to see and feel and hear with renewed amazement: "the Word became flesh and dwelt among us, full of grace and truth."

Thomas H. Troeger
Iliff School of Theology

Chapter 1

Recapturing the Joy of Preaching

Truly, I tell you,
whoever does not receive the kingdom of God as a little
child will never enter it.

—Luke 18:17

When I was a boy growing up in Virginia, I looked forward to my annual trip up to our church's conference center in the Blue Ridge Mountains. It was a beautiful place for a child of suburbia to go and catch a glimpse of the hand of the Creator. A boy only had to open his young eyes to the wide expanse of mountains and woodlands and his young ears to the sounds of both bird songs and hymns to "be still . . . and know."

Yet, it was rarely *still* up there. I remember that it was a very busy place. There was a lot of motion and sound as the conferees walked frenetically between meeting places and a carillon chimed to keep them on schedule. The main auditorium was on top of a large hill and it took real effort to walk up there for the assemblies. Many would pause on the porch outside of the auditorium to catch their breath or to take in the view.

One morning after one of the sessions, I stepped off the porch and started to run down that hill with abandon. My body remembers the sheer excitement as I gathered speed, my arms lifted out like wings, and my legs working frantically to take me to the bottom of that hill. A sound came freely out of my mouth, uninhibited, clear, and full of passion and joy. It was work to go back up the hill in order to run back down. Yet, I did it again and again that summer. Since it was such fun, I thought it was well worth the effort.

After falling a few times and scraping my hands and knees, I learned some techniques of downhill running. I knew how to moderate my speed without losing the excitement of being pulled by gravity. I learned to improvise my patterns of movement into zigzags, circles, and diagonal lines. I experimented with different sounds and movements. Soon other boys and girls began to join me in the game, and they developed their own ways of playing. It was all done to enrich the experience of the Downhill Run.

THE BODY AS ENERGY SOURCE

That memory has animated my vision of what the act of preaching can feel and sound like. In recent years we have been encouraged to listen to our "inner child." Perhaps that is what I am doing and encouraging you to do. Remember your own "downhill runs," for I believe that effective preaching is filled with that kind of primal, childlike energy.

Energy is the raw material of the creative person. It is what distinguishes the art of the effective preacher. Of course, there are different moods and complex emotional overtones when one speaks sermons week after week in this situation and that. Yet I have found that most preachers hunger for ways to energize and enliven their own process of preparing and preaching a sermon. What we have forgotten from our childhood is the sheer joy of our physical lives.

"Physical" preaching is energetic preaching. It involves the whole body. It is fraught with the danger of appearing foolish but is also driven by the excitement of improvisation. The sound of the preaching moment comes deeply and fully out of that "run" through the sermon. Once we have stepped off the safe place of rest, we can never turn back. We want to try it again and again. We want to learn new ways of zigging and zagging.

MOVING BEYOND THE BLOCKS

It is inevitable that something will come along in our experience that inhibits or blocks this free and spontaneous flow of energy. Somehow we begin to adopt "standardized" ways of thinking

16

about our work and look for quick results. Much of our formal education helped us learn a collection of formulas that are supposed to help us get those results. It is a rare teacher who will challenge us to give up the niche we have worked so hard to find. Yet, that is often what we need. Niches quickly become ruts.

Once when I was in a graduate seminar in play directing, I presented an experimental piece of theater that I thought was pretty good. I was proud of the way I *thought* I had gotten my message across to my audience. Yet when my colleagues commented on my performance, it was clear that what had gotten across was "a sermon." They felt that I was "preaching to them," and they had quickly turned my experiment off. They certainly did not take it as seriously as I did.

In that moment of pain, I knew that I would have to work at growth. I had learned a system of arranging ideas to create a desired effect and was having difficulty getting past that formula. In fact, I had achieved a good deal of recognition and success by learning to manage this formulaic way of thinking. Now I had come to see how limiting it was. The fact was I had fallen into a dull routine of doing things because I was afraid of improvising and experimenting. It took a lot of work, thought, and self-examination to learn some new ways of thinking about getting my ideas across.

Paul Baker, the teacher of that seminar, once said:

> Growth is the discovery of a dynamic power of the mind. There is a long period of intense study, criticism, and self-examination. Directions are not easily found; words do not come easily; the growth process is of little immediate interest to anyone else. The stimuli to growth comes from within that person. It is fed by ideas and sensations from nature, books, works of faith, bodily movement. . . . It demands utmost extension of the body it inhabits.[1]

In order to "storm the niches" we find ourselves settled in, we will have to think about preaching in different ways, ways I hope to point you to in this book.

THE BODY THINKS

I hope you will learn to listen to your body. Your body "thinks" and imagines with you. Your body holds a rich storehouse of memories that are rarely tapped when you prepare to speak. It is often these physical, kinesthetic experiences which open up a direction for a sermon.

One woman in a class I taught was quite frightened about becoming a preacher. Her voice was muted when she spoke and she held onto her manuscript tightly. Her phrasing was broken and it was difficult to follow her line of thought. During an improvisation on the text she chose, I asked her to take on one of the characters in the "sheep and goats" passage in Matthew 25:31-46. When she had some difficulty in identifying where she thought she belonged in that passage, I asked her to assume the perspective of someone she would *like* to be. She immediately assumed the role of the Son of man who came to sit "on the throne." When she did that her whole demeanor was transformed. She began to speak clearly and with authority. She seemed taller and was definitely more animated.

Then I asked her to assume some other perspective in the story. Without thinking, she adopted the position of the sheep on the right of the Son of man. When she knelt there, she could not speak at all. Tears began to flow. We waited in silence. Finally, all she could manage to say from there was that she knew at last what the passage "felt" like. She risked appearing foolish in order to find her way into the gospel lesson.

When we discussed the exercise later, Vivian (not her real name) indicated how important it was for her to embody the actions of the passage in order to identify with it. When she later preached her sermon on this passage for the class, she had assumed an entirely different persona. More of the qualities of the text were coming through as she spoke the sermon. On the one hand, she retained the authority of the Son of man, but she also preached the sermon with empathy for those sitting before the throne. Vivian had learned to think with her body in order to find her way into the text and come out again speaking with authority and empathy.

THE INTEGRATION OF BODY, SELF, AND VOICE

Frank had a slightly different problem. He had plenty of authority when he spoke and that authority came through his booming "prophetic" voice. Frank's extensive education in literature and theology had opened up many paths and avenues in, around, and through the biblical texts he chose. Yet when he spoke his sermons, he came across as intimidating and domineering. No matter what the text was, Frank seemed angry almost every time he preached. Frank joined a preaching study group to see if his peers could help him find some new ways of communicating.

What Frank was looking for was a way to integrate his imagination into a style for speaking. In what little spare time he had, Frank wrote poems and short stories. Yet Frank was uncharacteristically shy when asked about his writing. When Frank overcame his embarrassment and read these stories aloud to the other members of the group, an entirely different presence emerged. The Frank-in-the-stories was descriptive, playful, humorous, and vulnerable. We all agreed that these were qualities that Frank-in-the-sermon could certainly use.

After great effort, Frank began to find his voice for preaching by listening to this unauthorized version of himself. He understood how to be aware of his reader as he wrote. Could he do that as he prepared to preach? Frank adopted a technique of preparation that he hoped would help. Before he prepared the final draft of his sermon, Frank would begin to "talk it," that is, begin to compose *orally* before setting it down in writing.[2] He would stop and describe a setting or a character, filling in particular details and images. All the while, Frank held in his memory the research he had done in the library on the passages. Soon, the Frank-in-the-stories met the Frank-in-the-sermons. An amazing and exciting amount of creative energy was released as these parts of himself were integrated.

Frank recently sent me a videotape of one of his sermons. Instead of an angry persona in the sermon, I saw someone who was truly enjoying the preaching moment. He had decided to become more aware of his listeners by leaving his prepared manuscript in the study (though he still wrote one out each week) and by stepping out in the space between the pulpit and lectern in his church. It seemed very risky, as if the gravity of the sermon were pulling him into it. Yet that space became charged with Frank's own energy and enthusiasm as more of Frank "came through" in the preaching moment. Frank's strong voice had become a versatile instrument for evoking a wide range of emotion as more of him had become available in preaching. His sermons had become populated with characters he had held in his imagination for years.

NEW WAYS OF SEEING YOURSELF PREACH

If I were to choose a vision of preaching, I would select the image of Frank on that videotape or of Vivian in that classroom. Vivian had arrived at the preaching moment ready to allow the sermon to come through her. The text had not only given her an image of her own authority but also a vision of those who were oppressed by the world's authorities. The spoken sermon was a place where Vivian's experience of the Gospel came through her preaching persona. For me it became immediate, accessible, and demanded a response.

The sermon-in-performance was also a place of discovery for Frank. It was there that a long neglected part of who he was arrived and began to teach him how to speak his sermon. It was the fiction writer and poet in him that helped develop a more oral style and encouraged him to do in the sermon what seemed so natural in his writing—he developed a relationship with his listener. I would imagine that Frank's preaching has helped him improve his writing. I am confident Frank's listeners have come to trust rather than fear him now that more of his personal experience has surfaced in his sermons.

The most important discovery Vivian and Frank made was how to *enjoy* preaching again. They found a way to connect preaching with the Downhill Runs of childhood. They remembered that their bodies and other neglected parts of themselves were available to energize and inspire the preaching moment.

This book offers some suggestions on preparing for the moment when you will speak to your people in worship. It aims to activate a long inner conversation you will have with yourself, and it will invite you to listen to many voices. Some of these voices will be familiar, some forgotten, some never heard until now. I hope they will lead you along a path to more effective oral presentation of your sermon.

I hope you will find your own storehouse of energy, enthusiasm, and creativity. For if you do, there are a host of listeners on the hill who want to join you in the "run" to the Gospel.

Chapter 2

Effective Preaching Begins
with Self Discovery

*I only wanted to live in accord with
the promptings which came from my true self.
Why was that so very difficult?*

—Herman Hesse

In the first scene from Orson Welles's play *Moby Dick—Rehearsed,* a company of actors arrives at an old theater to do (as one of them puts it) a "sort of reading" of the novel *Moby Dick.* They are experimenting with the idea that they can capture the liveliness of the great story of Captain Ahab and the White Whale and stage it as a theater piece.[1] One actor, identified in the script as "an Old Pro," says, "My God, how can you put a thing like that on the stage?" Another actors adds, "This whale business was intended to be read!" And a younger actor replied, "To be read aloud. There are things in it that simply have to be heard!" The director arrives at the theater, assigns the appropriate parts, and the rehearsal is on. They are following an idea as big as the White Whale himself: the concept that the actors' voices and bodies can enliven an audience's experience of *Moby Dick.*

The preacher, sitting in his or her study on a Thursday night, may well have a similar concern when contemplating the sermon for delivery on Sunday morning. She may well look at the completed manuscript lying on the desk and wonder: "My God, how can you put a thing like that on the stage of the listener's imagination?" Plus, she realizes that both the text and the sermon have things in them "that simply have to be heard!"

The preacher, like the actors in the company of *Moby Dick—Rehearsed*, do not feel that their training has equipped them for such a venture. One of the actors longs to do a more conventional play, "something you can act." Another "Serious Actor" asks the director: "What exactly do you want me to *do* with my character?" The director replies: "Do? Stand six feet away and do your damndest!" The task for both preacher and the actors in this company is the same: to find a way of speaking the text that makes something happen for the listener. The problem is that neither the actor in the *Moby Dick* project nor the preacher feels prepared for the task. Like the Serious Actor, the preacher may be wondering, "What *exactly* do I do with this?" My hope is that this book will help preachers "do their damndest" in finding ways to speak their sermons more effectively.

THE PREACHER AS PRISM

Consider what you would like to see happen when you speak on Sunday morning. You would like to speak in such a way that the minds and hearts of the listeners are changed in some way. As you speak, you would like to become a witness to the Incarnation, so that God's Spirit would become flesh through the "words of your mouth and the meditation of your heart." You would like to be transparent to God's Spirit, a prism for God's bright and colorful Presence.

Every preacher longs for greater transparency in the pulpit. Every preacher yearns for greater congruity between who she is, what she says, and how she says it. As you sit in your study on Thursday, thinking how you will speak on Sunday, perhaps a cluster of painful images flash by in a brief millisecond of memory. Perhaps you recall the many times when you sat where the listeners sit and watched a preacher become contorted into a grotesque "false face" in the struggle to speak some good news. Sounds and sights in the sermon did not resolve the deeply felt puzzlement you brought with you to worship. Instead you became a witness to the arrival of a beguiling, disturbing presence which came through the preacher's wrestling match with God.

24

I remember one young preacher who brought a prepared reading of the 23rd Psalm to class. As the reading continued, the preacher's voice became harsh and his delivery more stylized. The gap between his own pleasant personality and his pulpit persona grew. His arms flailed about in repetitive patterns, and his eyes stayed fixed on the page. His own voice became louder as he responded to a set of inner voices that were, I suspect, telling him more about his role as a preacher than about what was in the text.

What the preacher seemed to be communicating with his voice and body was a state of anguished confusion about his relationship with God and his role as a bringer of good news. This young preacher had not taken the time to look again at his own experience. His "gospel" did not yet include scenes of "green pastures" or "still waters" or the awareness of God's comforting Presence in the shadowy places of life. Was this the way God acted in the valley of the shadow of death in his experience? Was this what God was suggesting to him as he preached? Or was he listening to some other voice from within?

We can all think of examples where a preacher talks about the love of God while showing us a pinched and furrowed countenance in the pulpit or speaks about comfort while wildly flailing arms, hands, and head distract and alarm us. Now in this moment before you preach, you may experience all of those images as a catch in your gut, and you humbly pray that this utterance on this occasion might be truthful, helpful, authentic. Perhaps you pray: "May the words of my mouth and the meditation of my heart be acceptable in your sight, O God, my strength and my redeemer." The psalmist's formulaic language expresses what you alone cannot: your desire to bring the resources of the ever-expanding fullness of your relationship with God to this moment.

THE ORIGIN OF GOOD SPEECH

Many books on the art of preaching wait until later to introduce the old character named "Delivery"; he is usually not consulted until all talk of composing the sermon is done and the preacher is impatiently concerned with how to speak what she has written.

"Delivery" (who comes from a distinguished family known as "Rhetoric") often takes the stage in the final chapter and is only allowed to speak about technique—stylistic devices such as enunciation, pitch, gesture, and volume.

The great teacher Aristotle preserved for us the earliest memories of Rhetoric's vocation: to help the fledgling speaker become more effective in the speech arts. Rhetoric's job was to answer the question, "How does the speaker *create* an effective impact" by discovering "all available means of persuasion?"[2] This emphasis on the creative function of speech restores rhetoric to his rightful place in the discussion. Rhetoric is more concerned about stimulating the speaker's creativity and imagination than about polishing her "style" or "ornament." If we listen to Rhetoric on his own turf, we will see that he does not begin with how the speaker sounds (diction) but who the speaker is (ethos). "The character (ethos) of the speaker is a cause for persuasion when the speech is so uttered as to make him worthy of belief."[3]

And so we will begin, as the ancients did, with the question of who you are. Some preachers may fear that learning skills in the area of presentation necessarily involves remaking themselves, becoming someone else. There is no denying that something unusual happens to you in the interval between sitting on the platform and standing up to speak. Donald Keough, president of the Coca-Cola Company, shares the following anecdote:

> More than thirty years ago, a Jesuit priest who served as my debate coach in college said that something happens to the human animal when he moves from a sitting to a standing position. A person who possesses the God-given ability to talk, unique to the human animal, and is normally articulate, becomes something less than human when he finds himself in front of an audience of more than two people. Something happens to the link between mind and speech, and for some reason he believes he has to project something other than what he really is.[4]

In order to speak well, the preacher must first be honest with him or herself, be able to take a hard look at how he or she gets any piece of work done, and then learn to "develop areas of (the) personality that in the past have been suppressed."[5] Becoming believable means dropping any phony speaking persona that you may have created and used over the years in order to become more fully who you are. The process of becoming a more credible speaker begins with looking and listening: to the deep interiorities of self, to the chorus of voices assembled in texts, and to the cries of the community.

THE PREACHER'S ORIGINS

Preaching can be artful communication; a sermon can awaken in both preacher and listener an appreciation of beauty, of mystery, of extraordinary significance. However, if the preacher is to become an artist, the preacher must demonstrate the artist's "concern for originality, meaning that which has origins and thus . . . build upon [our] own beginnings, [our] own potential."[6]

The origin of any piece of creative work of the imagination is in the creator's experience. The trouble is, most preachers have not been taught to become attentive to their own voices of experience. Most of the time, the preacher has worked hard to develop ways of getting a result and getting it quickly. All of us are aware of the growing body of literature that is intended to assist the preacher in "getting a sermon."

I was leading a workshop for a group of preachers. The first exercise was for each one to discuss how he or she was able to get a piece of work done. I asked the participants to describe the process they went through in preparing their sermons and to discuss what resistances they encountered in that process. One preacher confessed frankly that he did not *need* to spend much time on a sermon. He reported that he was part of an organization which sent him "sermon helps" every week, noting that it took a lot of the work out of his preaching. He was part of a new church start, he said, and felt it was more important to spend time making calls in the community than working on his sermon.

When I asked him why he had enrolled in the workshop, he said that he was looking for some new strategies for "bringing people in.'' He could not understand why his own way of working on the problem was not producing satisfactory results. This preacher was having a hard time being honest with himself. He was so eager to get quick results that he was bypassing some important personal issues in his ministry. I never heard this man preach, but I surmise that he was probably anxious and disconnected from himself.

We easily recognize this preacher's problem. We are all part of a culture which values quick results. Preachers have become consumers of those methods which will help them get results faster and more efficiently. As a result, many preachers do not give themselves time for original thought. These preachers are tempted to become copies of someone else. They have usually been taught to devalue their own experiences or at least are not given meaningful clues about how to incorporate those experiences into their ministry of preaching. Because they do not know how to approach the question of origins, many preachers become more imitative than creative.

A PARABLE OF DEVOTION

Brother John the Simple was one of St. Francis of Assisi's earliest disciples. Once John was out in the field plowing when he heard that Francis was in the village sweeping out the church. Everyone knew that Francis insisted God's house should always be clean and attractive. When John found Francis in the little church with his broom, he immediately picked up another broom and started sweeping too! John acted out his devotion to God by imitating Francis. Whenever they would stop by the road and Francis would reach down and rub his tired feet, John would do the same. If Francis raised his hands to heaven while praying, so would John. Julien Green notes in *God's Fool*, a biography of St. Francis, that the mentor was at first amused at John's imitative behavior but soon grew tired of it. When Francis reprimanded John for doing everything exactly as he did instead of finding his own way, John responded: ''Father, I have promised to do whatever you may do, and that is what I want, to do what you do.''[7]

This story reminds us that much of what we do in the pulpit is imitative behavior. The sounds and sights of our mentors are ever before us, even as we look for new ways to preach. Imitative behavior may have its own rewards; John the Simple was called "St. John" by Francis after John's death. Whenever we preach, we will certainly hear the echoes of preachers we have learned from.

But for the long journey from text, to idea, to sermon, to pulpit, to listener we need to return to our own origins, to the substance of our own stories. We need to take the time to walk over the terrain of our own experience, to drink from our own wells as they are fed by the streams of God. If we are to find these wells, we must be willing to develop what David Kelsey has called "disciplines of looking." One of my first teachers in the art of looking was a young boy on an old Virginia battlefield.

A PARABLE OF DISCOVERY

One of the great joys of my youth was digging for Civil War relics near my home. Mr. Wright, my seventh grade science teacher, had a metal detector. He would often go to a construction site in an area of the Petersburg Battlefield to skim the surface of recently turned earth for bullets, buttons, buckles—items which evoked our community's memories of the American Civil War. Since I knew that a metal detector was a luxury I could never afford, I asked him what advice he would give me for finding relics of my own. He taught me to have patience, to develop a keen eye for even the tiniest bit of rust in the raw earth, then to dig carefully in the detritus of several ages for what I sought. I was never very patient and I often wanted quick results. Since I did not take the time to develop my eye for detail, I was often disappointed in my search.

One Sunday afternoon I was walking over the mounds of earth turned over by bulldozers which were creating a space for a shopping center. I saw Mr. Wright in the distance, his eyes to the ground, sweeping first here and then there with his detector. Near me was a boy even younger than I. All he had to search with were his eyes and his hands. He suddenly stopped, got down on his knees, and concentrated on a tiny piece of rust sticking out of the clay. I looked, thought it was an old piece of pipe, and went on. He ran off and returned with his mother's gardening tools. Then he began to dig. Slowly, carefully, practicing some native skill for discovery, he recovered the object from the mud. It was a rifle, the kind used by a Union cavalryman in the siege of Petersburg, rusty but intact!

All of us who saw it were intoxicated with his joy. I will never forget the image of that young boy holding up his relic for all to see. "Look at what I found!" he cried out. "Look at *this!*" Even Mr. Wright came over to congratulate him on his remarkable find. I was left with the sound and sense of awe, embodied and expressed through that youngster. He had made a connection with our collective memory and had held it up for all to see.

The preacher is one who must go to the places where the earth is being upturned for good or ill. There, in the raw material of experience, the preacher must learn patience. If the preacher is looking for quick results instead of the bits of rust, she may miss what lies below the surface, a "relic" which evokes entire worlds of experience. Our best instruments for opening up the resources of our own inner terrain may be, as Paul Baker suggests, "learning to discover demands going inside of oneself, getting acquainted with all kinds of tracery, skittish little pictures and visions, bringing together experiences and memories that you have had . . . since childhood; you find them and realize them."[8]

Discovery requires some risk and some work. It means finding new ways of working that involve the sensory and emotional memory. The problem is that ministers have not been educated in institutions that encourage this kind of reflection. In an address to a consultation on the Arts and Theological Education at Candler School of Theology, December, 1985, David Kelsey offered this challenge:

> Patterns of theological education at least since the late sixteenth century have concentrated heavily on teaching students the necessary skills for critical conceptual work and have neglected teaching them skills necessary for disciplined looking. In the interests of being fair to the students' own humanity and in the

interests of equipping our students to provide leadership for Christian communities . . . it is incumbent upon us to help our students acquire the discipline of looking as well as the discipline of critical reflection.[9]

Preachers must first learn how to resist the temptation to work for quick results. The deepest connections between self and sermon are lodged in our interior landscape; they can be recovered only by taking the time to develop our capacity to look, listen, and remember in a cultural setting where memory has nearly become irrelevant. The joy comes when the "relics" are not only discovered but brought forth for all to see. Relics evoke awe in the listener because they give us an opportunity for experiencing the presence of "other": other times, other places, other people who are located in eternity. Our experience of Other begins as we look for relics from our own personal pilgrimages, memories that will lead us to a fresh experience of our origins. This is where originality begins, by recovering our own "relics."

DISCOVERY MEANS "SEEING AGAIN"

The playwright Lillian Hellman begins *Pentimento*, her book of memoirs, with the following image:

Old paint on canvas, as it ages, sometimes becomes transparent. When that happens it is possible, in some pictures, to see the original lines: a tree will show through a woman's dress, a child makes way for a dog, a large boat is no longer on an open sea. That is called pentimento because the painter "repented," changed his mind. Perhaps it would be as well to say that the old conception, replaced by a later choice, is a way of seeing and then seeing again.[10]

This image of the canvas reminds us that any creative act begins with an empty space. Before we do any piece of work, we have to think about our relationship with space. What is the first thing you feel like doing when you sit down to do some work? If you are going to write something down, you have to find a clean sheet of paper. You probably do not want paper which is cluttered with someone else's ideas.

If you come into your study and things are scattered here and there, you probably feel like picking them up and getting your desk straight before getting to work. We all have our favorite kinds of spaces—that clean, dimly lit room we like to rest in, the organized (or disorganized) protected private space of our office that we like to work in, or perhaps we like to be in busy spaces where there is a lot of stimulation. Many people are distracted from doing a meaningful and rewarding piece of work because they have not learned to establish a clean, empty space for doing that work.

When we *find* that kind of physical location for working, we usually learn how to be more present and attentive to what emerges from our inner spaces. Many times we are at a loss for a way to describe the images that show through the canvas of our personal experience. Remembered images may present themselves in a variety of ways: as rhythms and sounds, as colors and textures, or as lines, directions, and silhouettes. Learning how to translate image into word so that it can be shared in the faith community is one of the great joys of creative preaching. The elements of space, rhythm, and sound—or line, direction, and silhouette—offer ways of seeing and seeing again the images from our own experiences. They evoke the desire to recover those experiences and then to speak well about them.

Take a moment to see again a favorite childhood space. Where was that special place? Was it under the house? Was it a corner of the attic? Was it a tree house? Was it a place you and your friends cleared out in the woods? Was it under a piece of furniture? Think about what kind of space that was and how you were involved in it. How did you like to be in it physically? Were you active or still? Alone or with someone else? What kind of activity did you engage in while you were in this space? Did you read? Or did you invent games for yourself? When did you like to visit this space? In the daytime, or later during the night?

In thinking about this space, you were using techniques that help us recover our sensory memory. For example, you could simply recall the rhythms associated with the space. Were they slow, frantic, even or erratic? Were there long intervals between the sounds? Was there a good deal of silence in that space? Did you hear other voices? If so, what were the rhythmic qualities of those voices? What sounds did you make while you were there? Did you talk to yourself or were you quiet? Rhythm and sound is one way to open up dimensions of experience you might have forgotten.

The novelist Thomas Wolfe in *Of Time and the River* describes one of the great auditory experiences of childhood:

> But now the train was coming. Down the powerful shining tracks a half mile away, the huge black snout of the locomotive swung slowly round the magnificent bend and flare of the rails that went into the railway yards of Altamont two miles away, and with short explosive thunders of its squat funnel came barging slowly forward. Across the golden pollinated haze of the warm autumnal afternoon they watch it with numb lips and an empty hollowness of fear, delight, and sorrow in their hearts.[11]

Remembering a sound like this or a strong rhythm can unlock what F. Scott Fitzgerald called "the exact feel of a moment in time and space"[12] in our consciousness.

Another way to retrieve our memories of place is to think about line or silhouette. Paul Baker, a teacher and theater director from West Texas, remembers:

> In front of our house ran Twenty-Five-Mile Avenue. It ran straight for twenty-five miles, right to the edge of the horizon and right out of it. The road was one good, strong direction; unequivocally, one big strong line, which on hot days had mirages dancing on it, seemingly great puddles of water, and on windy days was filled with dust and tumbleweeds. Nevertheless, it was a line, a direction, static rhythm, a place of movement, a place for the drama of the various seasons. The drama was told by the people who traveled on it. It was a dirt road.[13]

Reading about or listening to others' childhood experiences of space, sound, or line remind us of our own primary experiences of being connected to our world, before, as Paul Baker says, we had "words to put the feelings together, or words to destroy the feelings.''[14] When we reflect on our own sensory experiences using these elements, we can see and hear the experiences again and again and discover a source of energy, power, and inspiration. Most important, we are rediscovering what it means to be human and involved in Creation.

THE PREACHER FEEDS THE FLOCK

To be human is to eat. To speak is to offer ''food for thought.'' It is interesting to note the way congregants use the language of the table to talk about their experience of listening to sermons.[15] They enter into the sanctuary with a sense of anticipation, describing themselves as ''hungry'' for a good sermon. Sometimes they may leave a service and even change communities because ''they are not being fed'' where they are. Preachers may scratch their heads and ask: ''What is it that my people are hungry for? How can my sermon be the substance God uses to satisfy their yawning appetites?'' I offer the following as an image for this task.

In the magnificent movie *Babette's Feast*, a demure French expatriate asks her two Swedish mistresses if she might be allowed to prepare the meal to celebrate their father's 100th birthday. Their father is revered by people in their village as a spiritual master and a small, aging, eccentric community has developed to follow his teachings. Lately the fabric of the group has been frayed by bickering and dissension.

Babette wins a lottery and spends all of her winnings in preparing the feast for her friends. At first, they are afraid they might violate the austere teachings of their master if they eat and drink the exotic fare this foreigner has prepared. As they eat and drink, however, they begin to embrace each other and gradually accept the gift of fellowship and rediscovered joy that Babette's artistry has made possible.

The preacher's ''food'' comes from his or her reasoned and imaginative engagement with Scripture, tradition, and the wisdom of the community. Yet the place where the feast is prepared is within the preacher's experience. When Babette offers what she has prepared from her native land, she is quietly offering herself. One of the beautiful aspects of the movie is seeing how Babette's offering of food evokes talk around the table. Gradually, as night falls, the lights in the simple dwelling burn brighter and the people at the table begin to tell their personal stories. What we hear is the sound of "night speech" drifting out of that dwelling; it is a very reassuring sound to the audience and reminds us of our own hungers for "night talk."

"Night talk" usually takes the form of stories. Storytellers in all cultures prefer to tell a tale at twilight, in that luminous, liminal time between the table and the bed. Which one of us has not had the gift of a story given to us by a parent or grandparent when we prepared to sleep? Which one of us does not at some time experience a twinge of regret that the television set has displaced the storyteller as the one who speaks just before we fully enter into night? The choices we make about who we allow to speak to us before we fall asleep reveal a lot about who we are as individuals and as a culture.

Storytellers, according to Robert Wilhelm,[16] understand the difference between "day talk" and "night talk." "Day talk" is concerned mostly with gathering data, drawing conclusions, and sharing ideas; "night talk" is focused on images. "Day talk" is conversation about meaning; "night talk" is the conversation itself. As night falls, storytellers offer those images which will help the listener dream a world. If the listener learns how to pay attention to those images, then the listener finds an avenue for self-discovery. Most of us have been taught that this "night talk" is "only dreaming" and are encouraged not to pay much attention to the language of dreams. In some cultures, however, the language of dreams becomes a strategy for meeting the day. For example, the Senoi people of Malaya begin the day by telling the stories of their dreams using the images of the dream to shape their stories. Elders in the tribe draw conclusions about tribal life from these dreams and instruct the tribe to act accordingly.

For many in our culture, the preacher provides the only access to sacred stories that the listener will have during the week. How can the preacher, who usually speaks just before high noon, lead a listener into the night as the storyteller does at twilight?

THE PREACHER AS ONE "ACQUAINTED WITH THE NIGHT"

A story leads the listener into other worlds, other times, and other realms of experience to grant the listener a fuller sense of self and world. This is the substance of the storyteller's art. That is why the storyteller is not afraid to enter into "night." "Night life" helps us to live in the light of day. Preachers must become, like the persona of the poem by Robert Frost, ones who are "Acquainted with the Night."

In the depths of the experience of Night, the solitary figure in the poem learns to expect, even if he or she continues to be surprised by, the in-breaking of Other.

This expectation is what gives the preacher the courage to enter into the Night of his or her own experience and that of the congregation. The preacher who is not afraid to stand still in the darkness and look and listen for the sounds and visions of the Other will be the one who hears the cries from great distances and sees the luminescence of the ordinary. This is the kind of preacher who will be able to lead a listener through the experience of Night and to transform it from a place of aloneness to an encounter with the Holy.

"HE CAME TO JESUS BY NIGHT AND SAID . . ."

One of the most famous encounters in John's Gospel is that between Jesus and Nicodemus. The Pharisee receives instruction from the Teacher about "new birth" . . . at night (John 3:2ff). The recurring motifs of light and darkness and day and night in John's Gospel are interwoven with images of bread and water. When Jesus meets Nicodemus, it is against the backdrop of the Passover feast. This is John's way of reminding us of humanity's hunger for signs that God is with us. Which one of us would not acknowledge that at this time of rapid change in social, political, and ecclesiastical spheres, we hunger for a fresh encounter with Christ? The preacher is the one who dares to go to Jesus by night and ask the question on each of our hearts: "How can a man or woman be born when they are old?'' Hopefully, the Word the preacher brings back from this nighttime encounter with Jesus will address our hunger for a sign from God. How might the preacher go about looking for Jesus "by night"? In the following poem by e. e. cummings, the persona has the kind of encounter we seek:

> No time ago
> or else a life
> walking in the dark
> i met Christ
>
> jesus) my heart
> flopped over
> and lay still
> while he passed (as
>
> close as i'm to you
> yes closer
> made of nothing
> except loneliness

Read the poem aloud. Write out your own reactions, questions, and reflections. Note first what the poet's sense of time is. He creates the impression that we are somewhere between real time (the existential time of "a life") and fairy tale time ("no time ago" suggests the formulaic opening of fairy tales "once upon a time.")[17] The juxtaposition of these two ways of talking about time, taken with the use of short, direct sentences, underscores the seriousness of the subject. It is a reminder to the preacher from the poet that the well-crafted short opening sentence can be richly evocative—that less is more. We are already on the threshold between the concrete ground of lived experience and the imaginative terrain of myth.

Now note *how* the poet talks about this experience by looking at the spacing of "i met Christ/jesus)." The sobering overtone of meeting Christ is balanced by the colloquial "jesus) my heart/flopped over/and lay still/while he passed." The image of Christ "passing by" evokes for me Mark's story of Jesus walking on the sea at the fourth watch of the night (Mark 6:45ff). In this story, Jesus means to pass the disciples by (v. 48b) but, as they are frightened, he gets into the boat with them. Here is the opportunity to reflect on those times in your life when Jesus came walking to you by night. What was the nature of that encounter? Was it one of fear? Or did your heart flop over and lie still?

One thing you will experience when you read this poem aloud to someone else is that the line "as close as i'm to you/ yes closer" creates an intimacy between you and your listener. It is difficult to speak these lines without a spirit of humility and awe. It is the way to speak of our encounters with Christ. Our style of speech about such matters should follow the example of this poet: it is personal and humble, naive, yet serious. As one of cummings's critics puts it: "By means of such a delicately responsive stylistic instrument, Cummings naturally avoids pomposity and inflated holiness."[18] Let us all aspire to this kind of work when crafting and speaking our sermons.

The final images of the poem leave us asking a question: who or what is "made of nothing except loneliness"? As I listen to the poem, I am inclined to think that the speaker's heart is what is made of nothing but loneliness. Perhaps loneliness, an active condition of longing for companionship, is a *substance* which makes up the heart. But as I look closer at the poem, I note where the parentheses are placed. One occurs after "jesus." It is the grammatical mark that is usually used to *close* a phrase. It invites us to ask where the parenthetical phrase might begin? The phrase beginning with "as close as i'm to you" is marked with an opening parenthesis. Our usual way of *seeing* this kind of construction on a page might be:

> (as close as i'm to you
> yes closer
> made of nothing
> except loneliness
> jesus)

If this is a valid way to treat the poem, then "jesus" is associated with loneliness. Our lingering final impression from the poem is of Jesus, fully involved with the human condition and seeking companionship . . . at night.

What this poet presents to us is a way of narrating his experience of meeting Christ at night. Cummings loosens traditional language, phrases, and images from their usual moorings in convention and thus opens them up for fresh interpretations. What emerges in this blend of the existential and the fantastic is a sense of what it is like to encounter Christ. Traditional ways of reflecting on Christ are juxtaposed with colloquial speech. While we can detect these stylistic devices by looking at the page, we cannot fully share in the experience narrated until we have heard the poem spoken.

I would like to return to the theater where the actors are preparing *Moby Dick—Rehearsed*. Before he begins the rehearsal with the entire company in Act 1, the director is instructing a young actress who has arrived thinking the company will be rehearsing Shakespeare's *King Lear*. "How now, Cordelia" quotes the director, "mend your speech a little, lest it may mar your fortunes." He then proceeds to sit on a throne and instruct her where to sit, how to stand, what inflections to give her phrases, and what movements to make. We, of course, lose all the beauty and poetry of the text in this technical instruction.

That, we find, is the point of the play and is also the point of this book. Most preachers have a mental image of a "director" sitting on a throne and instructing them how to speak "properly." What is lost is the beauty and grace of who they are and what they have to say. This book takes a different point of view about where to *begin* the process of finding effective ways of speaking the sermon. Finding a natural style for speaking a sermon begins with finding the preacher's own voice. The authentic sound that a preacher makes comes from the interrupted cries within the unexplored recesses of the preacher's own experience.

EXERCISES

The following exercises are designed to help you integrate what you are reading in this book with your own process of sermon preparation. They may be done with your preaching peer group or on your own.

One day while Mircea Eliade, the great teacher of world religions, was writing at his desk, the frame of his glasses broke.

He tried desperately to fix the frames, then wondered why he should try to preserve those old and somewhat ugly glasses. He was filled with a strange sense of sadness and longing. That is when he remembered that this pair of glasses was all he had left from his native Rumania. He realized that he had *nothing* remaining from his past, no plates, no books, no manuscripts, notes, pictures of his parents or himself as a child—everything was gone. There were no souvenirs left.[19]

Keeping a journal is one way to recover your personal relics or souvenirs. It is one way to begin cultivating a rich, inner dialogue with yourself and to discover how you really think and what you want to share out of your being.

This journal will be not simply a record of your experiences but an exploration of them. The following suggestions are intended to prompt this way of thinking.

1. Your first entry might be a description of your childhood space. Fill out the images which emerge in that memory and pay particular attention to your memories of your body and voice in that space. Translate this experience into speech by sharing it with a study partner or member of your preaching study group. Record (using pen, video, or audiotape) what happens to your voice and/or body when you orally share this experience with someone else.

2. Answer the following set of questions in your journal or orally in your group as a way of examining your origins:[20]

   a. Where was your hometown? Describe it as fully as you can. Pay attention to the rhythms you recall. What kind of spaces do you remember? Do you remember any experiences associated with the silhouettes of objects against the sky? For example, Paul Baker remembers

   the dramatic silhouette of the windmill . . . at a distance; the windmill, which brought water to our house, as it sat in the backyard impressed against the sky. On moonlit nights or in dust storms, barely visible, or on beautiful spring days when the weather changed from warm sunshine to a blizzard in only a few minutes, there was that windmill. Every kind of weather and wind and cloud silhouetted that windmill—lonesome, stark, friendly, grotesque.[21]

b. How was your home heated? Locate the center of warmth in the house. Was it a furnace? Fireplace? Gas heater? Wood-burning stove? What experiences do you remember that surround this center of warmth?

c. *Who* was the center of warmth in your home? Your father, mother, grandparent, sibling? Can you tell a story associated with your family's center of warmth? Can you give a physical description of this person or persons? Can you recreate a characteristic gesture or the sound of his or her voice?

3. Give a brief speech of about five minutes on the subject of your personal gospel. As you speak, try to identify which parts of your body are most animated or active. Your head? Your gut? Feet? Hands? What parts of your body are *uninvolved* when you speak? Chest? Eyes? Shoulders? What are the implications of this inventory for your preacing?

Chapter 3

The Power of Your Own Story in Preaching

I [Paul] think that I am not in the least inferior to these superapostles. I may be untrained in speech but not in knowledge.

—2 Corinthians 11:5–6

If you want to see and hear what our electronic culture considers to be good preaching, turn on the television set and watch one of the many evangelists present his message. (Unfortunately, as of this writing, I have yet to *see* a woman preaching on television!) Take note first of the setting of the sermon. Some evangelists are in a beautiful chancel area, some are using pulpits (note the *transparent* ones) and some are not. When they speak, they are full of energy and conviction and make free use of their bodies. They establish eye contact and their voices are well modulated, if they are not straining for effect. Directors of these programs are careful to include reaction shots of attentive listeners. Furrowed brows, smiles, and other nonverbal signals in the audience suggest that their attention is focused on what the speaker is saying and give you the impression that you are part of a large group of listeners.

Other evangelists are in a study with an open Bible. In the background are shelves of books, impressive symbols of authority. They look into the camera and appear to be talking directly to you, the listener.

Whatever our own opinion about the appropriateness of electronic media for proclaiming the Christian faith, one has to agree that the institution of electronic evangelism is demonstrating remarkable staying power in our culture. Critics may ridicule evangelists for moral indiscretions or despise them for their fund-raising practices. This evangelist or that one may even be discredited in the eyes of the public. Yet there always seems to be another one waiting in the wings, ready to refine his predecessor's use (or abuse) of the media and restore the popularity of television preaching. There seems to be a consensus among television evangelists that those preachers who use electronic media effectively are the ones whose influence upon our culture will be the greatest.

We are only beginning to assess the impact that electronic evangelism is having on the evolution of the church. Yet every pastor knows that the success of these evangelists in gaining and holding an audience has raised personal and professional issues for him or her and at times has dominated the discussion of how the faith is to be communicated. How does the preacher find his or her bearings in this bewildering electronic age? What are some trustworthy standards for good speaking? Does the biblical tradition lend any clues to the preacher in her or his struggle to speak with authority and authenticity from the pulpit? Do we all have to fit into the mold of the electronic evangelist in order to gain a listener's ear?

Thomas Boomershine, author of *Story Journey: An Invitation to the Gospel as Storytelling*, has noted in a lecture that the form of media that dominates a particular culture shapes the ways that the biblical stories are *experienced*. When I attended seminary, only one medium, print, was used to prepare ministers for communication in a multimedia world. Students for the ministry listened to lectures and took notes in silence, read the texts in the silence of libraries or the home, wrote papers in silence, and then even prepared sermons in silence. The process of sermon preparation usually produced a manuscript, and the student was given very little guidance on how to speak it. In fact, there was little opportunity for the student to stand and speak about what he or she had learned. Sermons were judged for their content, not for how they sounded or looked when the student spoke them, and feelings were considered suspicious ways of apprehending the Gospel.

Seminaries were preparing ministers for a world in which church members read the biblical stories in silence alone at home and came to church to join classes and study groups where theological ideas, extracted from the texts, were discussed and elaborated upon. A sermon was expected to be theologically well grounded but, when spoken, to sound like an essay being read.

What seminary students and pastors were beginning to find out, however, was that the world of silent print was quickly disappearing. A culture of print had changed into an electronic culture. The person sitting in the pew was not spending much time reading anything in silence, not even the Bible. He or she might be tuning into a particular Christian radio or television program to "get spiritually fed" and then making judgments on which speaker was more theologically correct than another. The person in the pew was getting more information about how he or she was to live from oral and visual media than from print. After learning to accept highly expressive and emotionally spontaneous communication styles on radio and television, the listener was coming to church to hear a preacher read scripture lessons and preach without much feeling or expression in the voice or body. Both the preacher and the listener seemed frustrated at being caught in this transition between media worlds.

Preachers found themselves looking for a manner of speaking that fit the demands of this electronic age but also a style which reflected their own personality. Listeners longed for preaching that was expressive, spontaneous, but substantive and personal. Many people left churches which were bound by the values of silent print culture for churches that were more "alive" with energetic and enthusiastic proclamations.

This is a complex issue which deserves more attention than I can give it here. What we must realize is that television and the other electronic media are defining standards of "good speech" in our culture. Those speakers who communicate with energy, conviction, emotion, and who establish contact with their audiences are having a greater impact than those who speak as emotionally detached commentators on events or ideas.

The standards of this electronic age are not new. Rhetoricians have always noted that the effective speaker is natural in her or his style and delivery. But how do you translate the passion you feel when conversing about an issue with friends into an effective style for public speech? This has always been the concern of rhetoricians.

In every age, both speaker and listener grope for what is natural in speaking. Aristotle expressed the heart of the matter ages ago when he said: "Naturalness is persuasive, artifice just the reverse. People grow suspicious of an artificial speaker, and think he has designs upon them—as if someone were mixing drinks for them."[1] What would a natural speaker look or sound like in our age?

We are all too aware of how media consultants and advertisers create powerful visual and aural images that manipulate our reactions to a politician or product. Preachers in the pulpit may deeply resist talk about creating "images," and that is understandable. The fact is, preaching (like any form of communication) is both a visual and aural event. When you meet someone, you immediately begin forming an impression on the basis of how that person looks and sounds. At times there is a startling discrepancy between a person's "look" and "sound."

A friend of mine recently attended a reunion of her husband's extended family in Texas. One of her husband's cousins walked up to introduce himself to her. He was a large man with a burly chest, strong arms, and legs like tree trunks. When she extended her hand to speak to him, she was surprised that this Texas giant spoke in a thin, high-pitched voice! From the moment he spoke, my friend's image of him changed drastically and she related to him differently.

Public speakers in any arena are becoming more aware of the messages their voices and bodies give when they speak and want their physical selves to serve the content of what they are saying. Whether we like it or not, the way we look and sound when we speak in the pulpit or in conversation conveys a particular impression of who we are to our listener.

Sandy Linver, author of *Speakeasy*, calls these important impressions "our spoken image," which "consists of much more than the words we say. It's how we say the words, the sound of our voice, the way we use our body as we speak—all of which determine how effectively we convey our message.''[2] Many may be suspicious of this image consciousness as a pathway into artifice. On the contrary, Linver notes that in developing awareness of your speaking image, your aim is to become the best of who you are, discovering and drawing upon hidden strengths in your style of speaking.[3] The Apostle Paul is a striking example of someone who became painfully aware of how he was coming across to his listeners and turned his personal weakness into strength.

THE APOSTLE PAUL AT CORINTH: AN IMAGE PROBLEM

Paul's Corinthian correspondence reveals that he had his hands full of problems in helping that church get established in one of the Hellenistic world's centers of culture. One particularly trouble-some episode was his conflict with the ''superapostles'' (2 Cor. 11:5) in the early 50s C.E. According to Dieter Georgi, these rival apostles were recognized as Christian missionaries who practiced and emphasized the significance of pneumatic activity in the life of the church, activities such as healing, ecstatic utterance, and recounting visions.[4] Paul's opponents attacked his credentials on many fronts, but perhaps the most devastating was the charge that his ''bodily presence is weak, and his speech, contemptible'' (2 Cor. 10:10). The word for presence is *parousia*, which means that, according to his opponents, Paul's very way of being in the Corinthian church communicated weakness. Likewise, his *logos* or speech was useless and ineffectual. Victor Paul Furnish in his commentary on Second Corinthians translates *logos* to mean ''a manner of public speaking.''[5] In short, Paul did not convey an impressive speaking image to the Corinthians. These other preachers had seized upon an area where Paul was vulnerable and were exploiting it to gain influence in the Corinthian church. We can imagine how difficult it was for Paul to admit that he was ''untrained in speech'' (11:6a) to the church where he had invested so much of himself.

THE SUPERAPOSTLES AT CORINTH: MODELS OF GOOD SPEECH

By contrast, Paul's opponents were obviously very gifted in some form of public presentation. We will never know exactly what genre of speech this was, but Georgi speculates that these "superapostles" were exceptionally gifted in the art of oral performance of sacred texts. Theirs was an age when "gospel" was an *oral* experience. Amos Wilder, a historian of rhetoric in the early church, gives us a clue to how the gospel was rendered.

> When we picture to ourselves the early Christian narrators we should make full allowance for animated and expressive narration. . . . Oral speech also was less inhibited than today . . . When we think of the early church meetings and testimonies and narrations we are probably well guided if we think of the way in which Vachel Lindsay read or of the appropriate readings of James Weldon Johnson's *God's Trombones*.[6]

The style of Christian storytellers did not arise out of a cultural vacuum; for nearly eight centuries a class of professional "singers" had refined a compelling oral art in Hellenistic culture. Since its nature was oral, it is difficult to reconstruct what it sounded like. Albert Lord and Milman Parry's book *The Singer of Tales* has become the foundation for studying this oral art. By listening to a class of folk singers (called *guslars*) in Yugoslavia, Lord and Parry concluded that the oral poets of preliterate Greece used formulas, that is, "a group of words which is regularly employed under the same metrical idea" to compose the narrations. The "singer of tales" accumulated these formulas throughout his career[7] and, in the act of utterance, created the story. Every performance was conditioned by the context of the utterance so that the length and emphases varied according to the demands of the occasion.[8]

Donald Hargis in his study of this tradition of recitation concludes that the "talk-song" from a modern musical comedy gives us an image for what these performances might have sounded like.[9] A better analogy from our culture is the art of the American folk preacher. Bruce Rosenberg has applied Parry and Lord's theory to his study of the "active oral tradition of the chanted sermon" in American folk culture. In the folk sermon, the language is ordered, the lines are metrical and poetic.[10] Thomas Boomershine, also a student of this oral tradition, is attempting to appropriate these insights into developing styles of biblical storytelling for the contemporary Christian community. His book *Story Journey: An Invitation to the Gospel as Storytelling* defines a process by which printed biblical stories are returned to oral, acoustical space.[11]

Christian storytellers were adept at setting the content of the story of Jesus within the oral forms of the day. Performances of these stories prompted a wide range of emotional responses from audiences. One sign of effective storytelling was the enthusiastic involvement of the audience. Storytellers would expect that the audience would *know* the story so that they could sing along, hum, or even accompany the tellings with musical instruments.[12] The story of Jesus when spoken and sung had the power to draw the community together.

While the majority of those in the Christian movement preferred orality as its repository for sacred stories, its leaders freely employed the art of writing. Texts were designed to capture the distinct features of oral discourse and encode them into written signs. In Christian worship, texts were returned to oral space by way of the public reader. The earliest description of Christian worship emphasizes the importance of listening to the reading and interpretation of sacred texts:

> On the day called after the sun a meeting of all who live in cities or in the country takes place at a common spot and the Memoirs of the Apostles or the writings of the Prophets are read as long as time allows. When the reader is finished the leader delivers an address through which he exhorts and requires them to follow noble teaching and examples.[13]

This practice of reading aloud in worship conformed to strong cultural conventions in the Greco-Roman world. By the time Cicero had become a dominant figure (106–43 B.C.E.), the custom of

reading literary works aloud in informal gatherings in Roman
homes was an established form of entertainment. Cicero wrote to
Atticus (XVI, 2), "I am sending you my *De Gloria*. Please keep it
as usual but have select passages marked for Salvius to read when
he has an appropriate party to dinner."[14] Not only did the poet
entertain by reading aloud at these welcome social events, these
gatherings were the principle media by which a poet might receive
critical attention for his work. So popular were these private
readings that they soon became more public and formal. Poets
began giving public recitals in temple libraries, museums, theaters
and wherever they could gather an audience in order to establish
their reputations as persons of culture. The practice was so
pervasive that by the time Paul was writing to the church at Corinth
(circa A.D. 50), satirists in Rome were complaining that "marble
halls are forever ringing until the pillars quiver and quake under the
continual recitations!"[15]

Poets who presented their works were keenly aware of the
competition for listeners and took their comments to heart in
revising their works. Pliny wrote of the importance of recitation to
an audience in the creative process:

> The reciter himself becomes a keener critic of his work, under the
> diffidence inspired by the audience. . . . He can discover his
> hearer's sentiments from the air of a countenance, the turn of a head
> or eye, the motion of a hand, a murmur of applause, or even silence
> itself; signs which plainly enough distinguish their real judgement
> from the language of civility.[16]

In spite of his use of oral recitation, Pliny did not consider himself
to be a good performer. In one of his letters, he asks a friend
whether he should use a freedman to perform some of his work,
concluding, "He will perform, I know, better than I can, provided
his fears do not disconcert him, for he is as unpracticed a reader as I
am a poet."[17] Pliny also wonders how he should conduct himself
during the performance:

> Now the perplexing question is, how shall I behave while he is
> reading; whether I shall sit silent, in a fixed or indolent posture, or

follow him as he pronounces with my eyes, hands, and voice; a manner which some, you know, practice. But I fancy I have as little gift for pantomime as for reading.[18]

This convention of arranging to have someone skilled in oral reading to effectively present one's own written work is instructive for understanding Paul's strategy against the ''superapostles'' at Corinth. Paul would be dependent on someone with oral skills to effectively present his letters to the Corinthians. In this highly charged competitive atmosphere, there were rigorous standards of excellence which governed public presentations of literature. Anyone desiring a hearing from listeners in the cultural centers of the day did well to heed these guidelines.

Those who taught ''good'' speech in Rome made certain assumptions of their pupils. First, they knew that their students had grown up in homes where recitation was valued. Second, they knew that recitation was deeply ingrained in the basic forms of learning. Finally, the teacher assumed that the pupil would bring certain ''natural'' gifts to the process. A pleasing quality of voice was essential to effectiveness.[19]

Next, the teachers of speech taught that the speaker had to thoroughly understand what was read aloud, spoken, or recited and be able to demonstrate that understanding. Before the student knew how to use the natural attributes of his voice and body, he first of all had to fully comprehend the text he was speaking and speaking about. When the student had a thorough knowledge of his material, he would then demonstrate it in the use of his voice and body. Both Quintilian and Cicero emphasized the importance of the voice and the gesture in helping the speaker express the emotional values of the material *and also* emotion which the speaker himself felt. If the speaker was able to empathize with these emotional values, then that speaker could arouse and evoke a response from an audience. To these Roman teachers of rhetoric, the basis for excellence was the *congruity* between the speaker's grasp of the content, use of gesture, and the use of the voice.

These principles were basic to all forms of speaking, public reading, and recitation and those who were able to master them had distinct social and political advantages. This appears to be the case in the conflict between Paul and the superapostles. In presentations of their oral gospels and in their readings and interpretations of texts, Paul's opponents had demonstrated their skill and command of these basic principles. In fact, they were holding this oral skill up to the Corinthians as a standard by which they should judge which of the apostolates should have authority in Corinth, those who could speak with power or the so-called apostle who was, by his own admission, "untrained" in speaking? The Corinthians had apparently been persuaded by the superapostles to use rhetorical skill as an index for a preacher's *true* knowledge. In order to win the Corinthians' respect, Paul had to shift the ground from technical skill in speaking to other kinds of "knowledge" (2 Cor. 11:6).

Paul uses the term *gnosis* to mean "the divine gift of spiritual insight."[20] According to the ancient rhetoricians, the effective speaker had to demonstrate knowledge of the soul. Here would be the proof of Paul's authority. If he could show such deep knowledge in his own form of self-presentation, Paul would be judged as a "natural" apostle. This would be his basis for "boasting in the Lord," not his skill in the oral arts. Paul's letter is a form of self-presentation that demonstrates the "weight and power" (2 Cor. 10:10a) of his insight.

PAUL'S LETTER AS SELF-PRESENTATION

Speech is a primary form of self-presentation. Any time we speak, we are revealing something of ourselves: our interests, our needs or concerns, our delights, and our intentions for action. Unless we are deliberately concealing something of ourselves, we try to say what we mean in order to get what we want. Sometimes we may not know or fully understand what our objectives are. We may be out of touch with our feelings and our way of speaking reveals it. The alert listener will pick up any discrepancies between what we say and what the physical or emotional parts of ourselves reveal. How many times have you said, "I feel fine!" to someone and then heard, "Well, you don't *look* fine!" Truthfulness in conversation demands congruity between *what* we say and *how* we say it. The same thing is true with any form of public speaking. To speak in public is to demonstrate concern for the same elements as speaking in conversation. We want to say what we mean, we want to use our bodies and voices to get our message across, and we want to be sure our listener gets the message we are trying to convey. It is absurd to think that we would try to assume another personality just to talk with someone across the aisle in an airplane. Yet many people think that in order to be their best self in public speaking, they have to imitate someone else! The effective speaker knows how to use the resources of his or her personality to achieve an objective, either in conversation or in the public speaking situation.

There are, of course, times when we fail. We have all had times in our lives when something happened in a situation that prevented us from getting our message across. Perhaps on those occasions we placed too much attention on the content of what we planned to say and not enough on the needs of our audience. Perhaps we paid too much attention to the audience and not enough to our authority as the speaker. When we are intimidated by the audience, we are likely to apologize for being there. The audience begins to wonder: "Well, why *are* you here?" Or perhaps we did not put enough time and attention into the message and we tried to "fake it," relying too heavily on personality to get a message across. In any case, we can all think of times when we failed to be our best with an audience.

I find that students at church-affiliated colleges or universities are among the hardest audiences to speak in front of. Many of these students are required to attend chapel services and come with deeply held resistances to the occasion. I was recently asked to speak to such an audience. It was a huge auditorium and the students were literally sprawled across the sea of noisy chairs in that expansive space. I stood up on a large empty stage and felt swallowed up when I walked out to face them. When I looked across the orchestra pit into dim light of the auditorium, I thought of Father Abraham's words to the rich man in Hades: "There is a huge chasm fixed between us and those who would go from there to here cannot nor can they go from us to you!" When I finished my presentation and walked off the stage, I could almost hear a collective sigh of relief that the ordeal of listening was over. I felt defeated by the occasion, humiliated, angry, and hurt that I had not found a way to reach them and to gain their respect.

That must have been a bit like Paul was feeling when he had encountered the ridicule of the men of Athens at Mars Hill (Acts 17:16ff) or during the "painful visit" to the church at Corinth (2 Cor. 2:1ff). When Paul was composing Second Corinthians 10-13, he undoubtedly wished that he could be in the church to personally respond to the charges leveled against him. Yet he was sensitive to his opponents' criticism of his skill in public presentation. They were clearly using his lack of expertise to draw attention to their own speaking abilities. What would happen if Paul returned to Corinth and spoke as poorly as he felt he did at Mars Hill? Paul had written to the Corinthians before and the form of the letter had proven "weighty and powerful" in the estimation of even his opponents. A carefully written letter when read aloud by an emissary who was skilled in oral presentation might make his case even better than Paul could make in person.

You, of course, are in a different situation. Paul resorted to writing a letter to his congregation when he was having difficulty speaking to them. You probably have to stand and speak in the pulpit next Sunday. How is Paul's experience helpful to you? This episode in Paul's troubled relationship with one of his churches illustrates the importance of the character of the speaker. As important as technique might be, the character and the trustworthiness of the speaker are more important. By all indications, Paul was not a talented speaker. Yet he was able to get his message across to a group of suspicious or even hostile listeners by employing the form of the letter. Paul's strategy at Corinth teaches some important principles for communication.

The letter was particularly suited for establishing the presence of an author to his or her reader. Ancient epistolary theorists note that the letter is designed to extend the possibility of friendship between parties after they have become physically separated. A friendship was dependent upon the "presence" of parties to each other. Thus, the fundamental structure of the letter—salutation, dialogue, and farewell—corresponds to the meeting between friends.[21] Deme-trius in *De Elocutione* states that "the letter ought to be written in the same manner as a dialogue, a letter being regarded by him as one of the two sides of a dialogue.''[22] The letter, according to Demetrius, was an important form of self-presentation.

The letter, like any dialogue, should abound in glimpses of character. It may be said that everybody reveals his own soul in his letters. In every other form of composition it is possible to discern the writer's character, but none so clearly as in the epistolary.[23] In Second Corinthians 10-13, we catch a glimpse of the ''character'' Paul intends to present the Corinthians, a multifaceted persona which reflects how Paul saw himself in relation to the Corinthian community. This presentation demonstrates some ground rules of excellence in communication.

Paul's opponents had made the mistake of trying to attack his personal character. Paul realized that he had certain limitations but had a strong image of himself as a knowledgeable person. The first rule of any effective communication strategy is that the speaker must develop a strong, realistic self-perception.

From the tone evident in the first chapter, Paul presents a strong, authoritative image of himself. Look at the words he chooses to address to his audience in chapter 10. If you read this letter aloud to yourself, you will be energized by his repeated use of strong verbal imagery. You will sense the strength of a bold, confident persona coming through. Is this the same Paul who is ''weak'' and has nothing substantial to say? The Corinthians, upon listening to his letter, must have been taken aback.

Audiences appreciate a speaker who will take charge of the situation and define the listening experience. Speakers whose choice of words and physical bearing suggest apology will command no respect or sympathy from an audience. Nor will an audience stay attentive when a speaker does not invest very much of him or herself in the presentation. You have been to enough professional meetings to know that when a speaker tries to ''objectify'' his or her presentation by ''just reading'' a paper or manuscript, you quickly tune out. I have often wondered why I have even gone through the exercise of listening to someone dispassionately read what he or she has written when I could have read it myself in silence and retained more information!

Paul realizes that his reputation is on the line at Corinth. He is the model for all speakers who know that a successful transaction between speaker and audience depends first upon that speaker's *personal* investment in that situation. Paul does not appeal for sympathy or make excuses, nor does he try to downplay his personal feelings. Paul knows that his authority is rooted in his experience with God and is prepared to use the full resources of his God-given personality to convey that conviction. What Paul did in the letter, we can do in a sermon.

Second, Paul is prepared to engage in some "serious play" with this letter. "Play" has always been a very effective and disarming device for lampooning social convention. There are a variety of forms of "play" given license in every culture; "players" will often assume some mask or disguise:

> Just as when tribesmen make masks, disguise themselves as monsters, heap up disparate ritual symbols, invert or parody profane reality in myths and folktales, so do the genres of industrial leisure, the theatre, poetry, novel, ballet, film, sport, rock music, classical music, art, pop art, etc. play with the factors of culture, sometimes assembling them in random, grotesque, improbable, surprising, shocking, usually experimental combinations.[24]

What is distinctive about Paul's "play" in this letter is the way he masks himself. Paul assumes the role of the "fool" (11:17). The concept of the Christian apostle as "fool" was intended to shock the Corinthian community.

Jesters and fools are permitted in every culture to rebuke authority figures by expressing "feelings of outraged morality." They may be priestly figures who temporarily "move out of their usual estate" in order to call attention to the foibles of the community. The function of these figures is to embody moral values against the "coercive power of supreme political rulers."

Such symbolic figures abound in the folk literature of many cultures. Variously called "holy beggars," "third sons," "little tailors," and "simpletons," they "strip off the pretensions of holders of high rank and office and reduce them to the level of common humanity and mortality."[25]

The touchstone for Paul's "foolishness" is what scholars have termed the "Fool's Discourse" at the heart of this letter

(11:1–12:12). Paul alerts the audience that he is playing the fool, (2 Cor. 11:1; 11:16; 11:21a) with all the rights and privileges afforded to these familiar, congenial figures, to make fun of the social structures imposed upon the church by the superapostles. Paul was a tent-maker, he and in order to make a living he would have set up shop in the marketplaces of his day. There, in the marketplace, Paul would have seen the performances of theatrical troupes which traveled throughout the Hellenistic world. A standard part in the repertoire of such troupes was a slave actor who would mask himself as a fool to ridicule authority figures. If Paul's opponents embodied the standards of performance exhibited by the professional oral poets of the day, Paul's counter-performance at Corinth was reminiscent of the troupes of fools in the marketplace. In performance, the "weakness" of fools became strengths derived from insight and high purpose, a lesson which Paul puts into practice in composing this letter. Paul is not afraid to cast himself as a fool in dealing with the Corinthians because in doing so he exposes the pretentiousness of his opponents and the folly of the Corinthians in accepting their exaggerated claims.

Finally, the letter reveals that Paul has the capacity to be open about his own personal experience, casting it in the form of a narrative. Paul is not known as a storyteller and chapter 11:21b–12:10 is not put forth as an expert's offering. In fact, theologian Tom Driver says: "If we compare Jesus with St. Paul, we may notice that while Jesus is a master storyteller and teaches hardly anything without a parable, Paul has turned the whole of history into a saga notoriously lacking in humor and irony."[26] It was not only the ancient Corinthians who had trouble seeing Paul as an oral storyteller! However, Paul does show that what he lacks in technical skill, he makes up for in knowledge of the soul. You don't have to be an expert to use your story effectively. This personal narrative reveals not only Paul's concept of Christian ministry but also his understanding of human existence under God. How Paul uses his own story in his struggle for apostolic authority is important here.

I am always surprised at the difficulty our incoming seminary students have with telling their own stories. It is not that the students are reluctant to talk about themselves. Many are ready to supply narrative material informing us of their background, and this material has value. However, as Tom Driver observes of his students:

> Most . . . will rely upon material exhumed in psychotherapy. Its virtue is that it is personal and has taken some pain to discover. Its fault is its blindness to the part played in all our stories by money, social class, tradition, and ideology. You would think, from most of the stories, that time flowed only through the nuclear family.[27]

I teach in a seminary in the southeastern region of the United States. Most of our students come from that region, most are white and from the American middle class (though we are fortunately seeing more African-American students and an ever-increasing enrollment of women, both black and white). I enjoy the rich variety of stories that emerge as students get to know one another, but there does seem to be a dominant personal story that surfaces whenever these students talk about their decision to enter seminary. It is an account of how their lives intersect with the Jesus Story. The plot goes something like this: the student grows up in the church (or in some close relationship with the church), then he or she "falls away," that is, the student's story and Jesus' are on different paths. Finally, in some kind of encounter, the individual "meets" Jesus and accepts a "call" to ministry. Some students do not share this kind of story and struggle to place their own stories within that dominant pattern. Their task is usually to critique that pattern so that they might be free to discover their own. Driver notes, "Christian teaching often compounds the problem by encouraging self-effacement, and by implying that the only story that matters is the one, big saga of the world's redemption."[28] One distinct advantage of cross-cultural communication within the seminary community will be the way dominant understandings of personal salvation and call will be challenged and enriched.

While these stories reveal some important presuppositions about their identity as Christian ministers, what interests me is how the students use the stories. They seem to reassure the student that he or she "fits in" to the seminary community, that there is a common "call" story they can all be a part of. Theirs appears to be a version of a story that has been verified and officially accepted by the church and they hold on to it faithfully.

One of the tasks of theological education, of course, is to help more of the student's story become available for reflection as a resource within the living oral, narrative traditions which are always flowing through the church. The hope is that the student will learn to be open to his or her own story as it unfolds, will learn how that story can become more fully available to the church, and by telling that story, will become a more attentive listener to other stories.

We are all aware of those who use their stories for other purposes. One woman who came through the seminary told a story of her miraculous healing and subsequent visions and special revelations. She told us that she had developed quite a ministry through telling this story in its many variants and had come to seminary to see how her experience could be integrated with others within the Church. She was a physically attractive woman, white, wealthy, and spoke with animation and vivid imagery. Her gospel very quickly set the agenda for the group's reflection. The others in the group found themselves positioning their gospel around the conceptual center she had established. It was clear that this experience was at the heart of her understanding of what ministry and the Christian life meant, but it had the effect of keeping her isolated.

The students in her peer group had a difficult time listening to her story. A wide variety of theological points of view concerning healing were represented but that did not seem to be a primary issue. What troubled this woman's peers in ministry was the way she *used* her story. It did not evoke from them their own stories of healing or joy. Rather, it made them feel uncomfortable with their own level of understanding, and therefore tended to make it even more difficult for them to tell their own stories. One man commented that the story she told pressured him to use "Christianspeak," that is, a way of talking about his experience that seemed glib and artificial. None of us felt we could argue with the veracity of her claims, but we certainly did not feel that our stories were evoked from *her* telling.

"Story" invites discussion of "plot"; and plot, according to

Aristotle in *Poetics,* is the soul of the drama.[29] When the pastoral counselor listens to stories of the one struggling for meaning and coherence, that counselor is hearing the resonances of the soul. When the preacher uses his or her own story in a sermon *effectively*, that preacher invites the listener to attend to matters of the soul, and not to the preacher's skill as a storyteller. The sign of effective personal storytelling is that it creates an atmosphere where other stories within the community's memory are evoked, not demeaned.

> The creation of a vivified present is the prime motive for telling stories, and this becomes even more important in religious communities, where stories go hand in hand with making music, performing sacraments, and doing rituals of all kinds. . . . Rightly apprehended, these activities do not glorify the past so much as they fill the present with power. It is as if the energy of all time were trained upon the present, charging it with meaning, and causing it to burst with potency upon the future.[30]

Paul records the story of his experiences to evoke the memory of Jesus and thereby establish the ground of his authority. He brings to mind images of suffering that the Corinthians had not been remembering. Paul would not have gotten the credibility he wanted by simply eliciting pity from his audience; instead, he successfully invited the Corinthians to participate by remembering a forgotten part of Jesus' story.

The power of the personal story to evoke other stories depends both on the teller's degree of self-knowledge and his or her capacity to enjoy telling it. Driver says: "There is a positive correlation between knowing myself and telling stories about myself, or telling any story."[31] It was this *gnosis* that helped Paul make his claim to authority, not his technique as a Christian storyteller. Paul knew himself, had a strong self-perception, and knew how to take on the role of a fool. This gave him license to tell his own story, not in a way that drew attention to himself or that silenced other tellings, but in a way that invited the Corinthians to remember Jesus.

The conflict between Paul and the superapostles is, in part, a conflict between two strategies of "good" communication. As in any crisis, deeply held values and principles for good communication surface and are revealed to the preacher in any age. Ancient rhetoricians taught that the effective public speaker understood the meaning of what they planned to say or recite. (Though this may seem obvious, it is also apparent that many preachers do not adequately study what the focus of their text and/or sermon is about before they preach!) Understanding leads to congruity between sermon, body, and voice. Listeners are distracted by any action, physical or verbal, that obstructs this communication of meaning. Public speakers who are able to empathize with the emotional values of a piece and are capable of embodying those qualities through voice and movement are "natural."

While the superapostles at Corinth embodied these notions of excellence, Paul's self-presentation showed that in and of themselves, these standards could not be used as an index for true "knowledge." In fact, Paul's letter reveals a more substantive basis for effective presentation. Paul grounded his claim to knowledge of the soul in:

1. possession of strong sense of who he was before God,
2. willingness to risk "playing the fool,"
3. openness to his own story as a resource for the community.

Even though Paul was not exceptionally skilled in telling his story, his letter allowed Paul to be effectively present in the Corinthian church. The test of a speaker's use of any media, oral, written, or electronic, is whether it demonstrates that speaker's knowledge of the human soul.

EXERCISES

1. For journal entry or discussion in preaching peer groups:

What do you think "good speaking" is?
Who models these qualities for you?
What are your strengths as a speaker?
What are your weaknesses?
What specific goals will you set for yourself in improving your
    speaking?
How can others help you achieve your goals for good speech?[32]

2. Tell a story about a time when you "played the fool." What did you enjoy about yourself when you were foolish? Watch others in your group as they tell this story. What happens to their voices and bodies as they tell this story? What kinds of inventive behavior does "foolishness" evoke?

a. Is there a time when sermon preparation or delivery becomes "play" for you? What could you do to restore playfulness to this process?

b. Watch the way a comedian or clown conveys truth to an audience. What vocal or physical qualities do these artists depend on? Now watch yourself on videotape telling a joke or a humorous story about yourself. How do you use those same qualities?

c. Give a one to two minute talk in the style of preaching opposite yours. Feel free to exaggerate and loosen up. If it is possible, capture this moment or two on videotape. Then play it back without the sound. What surprises you about the way you use your body? What did the "foolishness" release in you?

3. Reread the "Fool's Discourse" (2 Cor. 11:1–12:6) aloud and exaggerate the presentation. What things do you discover about your own story? What is your own catalogue of hardships in the ministry? Can you cast some of these experiences into stories?

4. Theologian Tom Driver says, "To become a person, and to be a growing person, is to evolve stories about oneself in which continuity and change are integrated."[33] Recall a story about a change in your life. It might be a time when you changed churches, careers, or even lifestyles. Recapture something "unfamiliar" about that story and exaggerate it. You might take another perspective than that of your own and recast the events of the story; you might further develop the images of setting by expanding them; or you might enlarge the presentation of other characters in your story. Write this story in your journal or orally improvise it to a group of listeners.

What is continuous in this story with other parts of your
    story? With parts of your community's story?
What represents real change?
How does this story affect your self-understanding and the
    way you want to look and sound when you preach?

Chapter 4

Establishing Congruity Between Your Personal and Preaching Persona

*Truth through personality is our description
of real preaching.*

—Phillips Brooks

Consider the situation of the pastor who wrote the following journal entry in a continuing education seminar:

> Throughout my ministry I have tried to preach sermons which would inspire a greater degree of discipleship among church members. . . . To be honest, I have had more failures than successes. The church I am now serving has encouraged me to try ₐand understand why my preaching is not effective. Though I have been loved and accepted by this congregation, I do not feel that my preaching has made any real difference in their lives. . . . It has been a painful experience to realize this but from the pain will come growth. The question is: how am I going to make this growth happen?

Any one of us could have written these same words at some point in our ministries. This pastor certainly understands what the goal of Christian preaching is. When "effective," it makes and remakes our identities as disciples of Jesus Christ. What he is having difficulty with is how to preach accordingly. What does the congregation mean when they indicate that his "preaching is not effective"? Do they mean that their pastor needs to make some different choices in his *style* of speaking? Do they long, for example, for more eye contact or for the pastor to speak without notes? Perhaps. No doubt that is part of what makes up their unacknowledged criteria for effectiveness. But what is the basis for this change in behavior? Will the preacher simply "put it on" like a new set of clothes? Suppose the pastor makes different choices but then looks and sounds artificial? Must we borrow our preaching styles from the marketplace without reflecting on our own theological and rhetorical traditions for doing so? The actual word *effect* points to something more substantive than technique and gives all preachers firm footing for making changes in the way we speak.

To *effect* means to "bring into existence" an intention or result. It appears that this congregation is waiting for something to be "effected" or brought forth in the speaking of the sermon that will create in them the desire to be disciples of Jesus Christ. The absence of this quality has caused pain in the ministry of this pastor and stasis in the ministry of the congregation. What could they be looking for? Paul Wilkes, in a sensitive observation of future church leaders now attending seminary, gives us a clue of what that might be.

> If they are to succeed, this generation of seminarians must, of course, be educationally and spiritually sound, politically aware, as conversant with demography as they are with morality. They must be sensitive to race, ethnicity, gender, and sexuality, but they must not drive us up still another wall with their convictions. We have been flogged enough; we know our shortcomings. When our future clerics speak, we want to hear powerful yet measured voices bringing out the moral dimension of life . . . We want them to be people who in some tiny way reflect the mercy and goodness of the God we want to know, not only his judgment. We want them to be people who see the goodness in us that we have yet to unleash, the potential within us to transcend our differences. In the end, I think, we are looking for those who will help us find that voice deep within us which is not our own but calls us to do what is right.[1]

There is an interesting interplay in Wilkes's references between those powerful and measured voices we long to hear from the pulpit and the "voice deep within us which *is not our own*" (italics added). Growth for this preacher and for the community he serves will come from discovering the connection between *his* voice for preaching and that inner voice which makes disciples of both pastor and congregation. If your voice for preaching is not yet a sounding board for the "voice deep within," there will be only dissonance and confusion among your hearers, not a call "to do what is right." Where does the path to this kind of growth open up? Aristotle believed that truth in speaking began with congruity between the speaker and the message.

RECOVERING THE ETHOS OF THE PREACHER

Aristotle struggled with the question of what made a speaker's claim seem truthful to a listener. He taught that the most potent means of persuasion was the ethos or character of the speaker. If there was no congruity between *what* the speaker was saying and *who* the speaker was in the act of presenting the speech, then that speaker was not credible or "worthy of belief."[2] One reason that Aristotle emphasized this attribute in his *Rhetoric* was that other handbooks of his day were devoted to technical rhetoric which, in Aristotle's opinion, established effective techniques for constructing and delivering speeches but paid too little attention to the role that the speaker's personhood played in persuading an audience.[3]

This point was brought home to me by one of my colleagues recently. When asked to introduce a popular preacher, he set aside his prepared comments about the preacher's degrees, publications, and credentials and instead took the time to speak about the preacher's integrity of character. By placing emphasis on *who* this speaker was, he prepared us to listen in a powerful way and made our experience of listening to this preacher's message more enriching. I was as moved by the introduction as I was by the address itself. Introduction and message were of one piece that "effected" in me the desire to become a better Christian.

Aristotle would teach that what prompted me to listen was the character or ethos of the speaker which my colleague drew upon in his introduction and which the preacher reaffirmed in his address.

Effective speaking is a transaction between the speaker and an audience in which an audience comes to trust the speaker and thereby accepts the speaker's message. My colleague told his audience that this speaker was first of all *trustworthy*.

Christian preachers take note: your congregations yearn for such trust. They bring this yearning with them to worship and to all other convenings of the community. Your listeners want above all to be able to trust you and to trust the Christian Gospel you speak of. To be able to engage them effectively, you must first trust yourself and your own understanding of Christian discipleship.

A guest preacher reminded our community of this in a recent homily for our seminary chapel:

> To what do we witness? Something that helps us with our anxiety in difficult situations? Something that overcomes our grief in the midst of pain? Some pleasant memory that will help us overcome the shock of being in strange and alien places? What the Gospel does is ask us to witness to the *effect* of the Resurrection, not argue the "truth" of it. Our people don't come to us and sit in the pew hoping we will condone their misery but in the hope that somehow what we witness to will light a spark in their lives that will help them find a better way.[4]

Your witness to the Gospel of a Risen Lord is what gives you your right to speak to your listeners and makes you capable of calling forth the barely audible voice of God within them. If you do not have a secure sense of self and conviction about your right to address your people, then it will be nearly impossible to engage them. Effective preachers are those who are credible witnesses to the Gospel and who communicate that truth to their listeners.

DISTORTIONS AND DISSONANCES IN MINISTERIAL CHARACTER

It is easier for a listener to decide who is effective than it is for a preacher to find the way toward effectiveness. All of us get lost on that treacherous path from time to time and need our listeners and peers to help us get back to being who we are. We tend to borrow mannerisms that attract us and appropriate methods and styles that come from outside ourselves when we do not trust those inner voices which guide our way of speaking.

As a speech teacher in a seminary, I am often confronted by student preachers who want me, as a specialist, to remake them into some preconceived image of the "effective" speaker, an image that eludes their grasp. They feel there is some generic standard of behavior they must "put on" in order to speak effectively. Even those students who converse naturally and easily in small groups suddenly become stiff and stilted in the pulpit. The primary task in teaching them is to encourage them to trust and enlarge those instincts and impulses that come naturally in conversation but are somehow censored when the student preacher is in the pulpit.

On the other hand, I regularly see students who have adopted and internalized patterns and mannerisms of "pulpit behavior," making it difficult to separate who they are from their characterisitics in the pulpit. These students have learned ways of speaking that were appropriate in some communities in their roles as preacher. Because they were successful in adopting these codes of behavior in their own communities, they attempt to transport this mode of communication to other settings where it sounds strange and unnatural. Moreover, they tend to hide inside these socially acceptable roles and have considerable difficulty engaging listeners in normal conversation. Their struggle is to risk stepping out of their role as preacher and to rediscover other instincts for communication that are available to them.

To help the students identify where they can improve their communication skills, we conduct a speech assessment exercise at our seminary for all incoming ministerial students. Each student is expected to prepare a five minute speech on a topic of his or her choice and deliver it for evaluation to a group of his or her peers. It is an opportunity to see firsthand how these students approach the problems presented by public speaking: what patterns students follow in preparing to speak, in organizing their thoughts, and in presenting them to a group are all observed and evaluated. Perhaps the most important part of the exercise is to see how the act of speaking reveals and/or conceals the personhood of each speaker.

On one occasion, a student gave a speech that was well organized, coherent, and delivered with a high level of energy. The student did not seem to be anxious or uneasy but moved smoothly through the speech with verve and polish. I could see that this young man was on his way to being an effective "technical" communicator. His voice and manner were pleasant, his gestures animated and practiced, and his control of the message was complete. He seemed to demonstrate the efficacy of standard, dominant models of speech communication. Eugene Lowry talks about those processes that are dominant in communication theory:

> During preparation you move toward the articulation of one propositional sentence that states unequivocally the theme you are going to address. In the speech itself, you begin with an introduction that identifies for listeners the exact subject to be covered. The theme is divided into three Roman-numeraled parts and is restated in a conclusion. . . . The art of communication (consists) primarily of transmitting a set of complete ideas from one location to another via the "conveyor belt" called speech.[5]

This particular student fully demonstrated the organizational values revealed in this model. Yet there was definitely something missing from his presentation which I could not yet name.

When he had finished, I brought my pen up to my pad to write down some comments for my report. I was stuck. I simply did not know what to write. I did not have the vocabulary I needed to critique him. I felt as if I had not really heard anything, that the whole experience of listening to him was a hollow one, and that he had sounded like hundreds, maybe even thousands of other "pleasant" preachers I had heard in my life. I thought first of Holden Caulfield's complaint in *The Catcher in the Rye:*

> If you want to know the truth, I can't even stand ministers. The ones they've had at every school I've gone to, they all have these Holy Joe voices when they start giving their sermons. God, I hate that. I don't see why the hell they can't talk in their natural voice. They sound so phony when they talk.[6]

I understood, however, that what I was hearing might well have been the way this student had been taught to preach! For his community and in its time and place, perhaps this mode of speaking would not be deemed "phony" but in fact as an avenue toward the sacred. How might I respect his manner and mode of speaking while challenging him to reveal more of who he was in what he said? It began to occur to me what was missing. He was speaking in a way that was characteristic of a number of preachers I had heard but did not offer much of his character as a human being. What was unique about *his* perspective? I could not tell, especially from his use of language.

The poet Wallace Stevens once told a group of students: "Nothing is quite as easy as using words like somebody else. We all of us do exactly this nearly all of the time—and whenever we do it, we are not poets."[7] Indeed, or preachers either. Yet it was not only an issue of what he said or did not say. It was how he had said it. His way of speaking seemed curiously inappropriate for this context. He seemed to be "borrowing" even his demeanor and style from one place and attempting to transport it to another setting in which it seemed practiced and predictable.

Apparently, I am not the only observer who experiences some preachers' public self-presentations as slick, mannered, and artificial. One writer who teaches English at a church-affiliated college made the following observations when she was in the company of a group of clergymen and women who were visiting her campus:

> There's a deadly sameness to the rhetoric, physical appearance, and conduct of believers who have official roles in any church. . . . From the moment a flushed convert enters the seminary, he or she runs the risk of travelling ever farther away from that first bright light of conviction and commitment, the moment in the corn field or the corporate office when God calls. Standardization is the curse of all institutional life, and it is next to impossible to hold onto the one true self—that individual, private miracle—in the face of enticements to promotion and prestige or the pressures brought to bear by conventional congregations who like a preacher to look, talk, and act like a preacher.[8]

Yes, this was a piece of it. He seemed "standardized." Was this mannered address one of the "curses of institutional life" this writer was railing against? Do those of us who hold official roles in churches look, act, and sound the same to those on the outside of our respective communities? All of us have had the experience of being in meetings and gatherings where we have found ourselves conforming to some implicit standard of behavior. We use language and code words that befit our roles and status and, to be honest, we admit to ourselves that "the first bright light of conviction and commitment" sometimes seems very far away in such meetings. How do we maintain the balance between "that individual, private miracle" that is ourselves and the "self" that is shaped by the communities we serve?

What is striking about this observer's disturbing comments is the assumption that the preacher's self, that "individual, private miracle," must somehow develop *outside* of the influence of particular faith communities. What she was experiencing is the embodiment of a particular code of behavior which has value within the faith communities which these believers represent, but a code of behavior that failed to engage her successfully and draw her out beyond herself and into relationship with them. In these particular communities, preachers who look, talk, and act in certain "standardized" ways are prized and even awarded prestige. What is the creative tension between who I am and the forms of public expression which are prized in the faith communities I represent? This was what was absent in my student's presentation: a tension between who he was and what communal role he embodied in his presentation. He seemed so clearly identified with the form of mannered expression his community of hearers expected that there was little room in his preaching for the emergence of other parts of himself. I finally found a point of identification with him. The reason why I had such difficulty critiquing him was that I had had a similar experience as a young minister.

Once when I was a ministerial student, my father asked me to fill in for him at his church outside the city where we lived. I was to lead worship and speak for him at the regular Wednesday night service while he was out of town. I remember the feeling I had standing up to speak to that gathered group. I knew what they were expecting to happen, and I knew from my experience as a public speaker how to accomplish it. I presented to them a message which contained all the right phrases in a well-ordered, coherent design. In fact, I received a favorable response from them. As they departed, they encouraged me to continue in my study for the ministry, for they assured me that I had potential and promise.

When I was alone with my thoughts on the drive home, I felt hollow and despondent. I realized that this message had not come out of my own, lived experience. The language I had used in my message was glib and riddled with generalities. I felt as though I had misled them. I had done what was expected of me, but I did not tell *or embody* the truth. I was so conversant with the form of self-presentation I felt the community expected that I lost touch with my own deep inner voice. In fact, I did not feel that this community would have accepted the real me in those moments. I was honestly struggling with the claims of the Christian faith in my life and trying to come to terms with my identity as Christian.

That community of believers would probably have allowed me greater freedom in revealing more of who I was than I was allowing myself. They might have needed my honesty as much as I needed their acceptance. We simply did not trust each other enough. I did not want this student preacher to fall into that trap. How might he learn to trust his listeners so that they might trust him? That was what was missing—a level of trust.

This personal story became the basis of my response to him. I sketched out my impressions in the form of an evaluation and sent it to the student. He made an appointment to see me to discuss my comments. In our conversation, I noted his deeply felt desire to shake loose of this artificial and contrived manner of speaking and try to find ways of being fresh and authentic in his presentation. He admitted that he felt trapped in a style that was "not him" and did not know how to be more "natural" in the pulpit. I told him that I had the same tendency.

It is easier to exercise the speaking skills we have learned succeed in the congregational cultures we are in than it is to find our own voice for speaking the truth. We are tempted to adopt an artificial persona[9] for preaching if we know it has "worked." Yet we sense that it is a hollow reflection of who we are, that it prompts us to borrow our words from others, and hence sound like everyone else. In that time of critical feedback, my student and I both discovered that we needed to identify those images of "effectiveness" that dominate our culture and the models of "good communication" which they generate. Then we needed to find some new ways of thinking about speaking the sermon; the ones that had once served us were proving to be inadequate in building trust.

THE POWER OF DOMINANT CULTURAL IMAGES

Joseph Hough, Jr., and John Cobb, Jr., have pointed out in a perceptive study entitled *Christian Identity and Theological Education* that the "manager" and "therapist" are the dominant ministerial "characters" of our time.[10] Drawing from Alisdair MacIntyre's *After Virtue*, they define "characters" as those dominant social figures that give definition to culture. Like the stock characters in the Japanese Noh dramas or the English morality plays, for example, social characters are immediately recognized by the audience. "Therefore, if one recognizes these characters, one can also readily interpret the intentions of the actors who play them. They are also central to the plot, and other actors always play their roles in relation to these central characters."[11]

We can see this principle operating in Paul's encounter with the superapostles at Corinth. One of the dominant characters within the early Christian missionary movement in the Hellenistic world was the "divine man missionary." When a group of these missionaries arrived at Corinth, bringing with them their letters of recommendation from other churches (2 Cor. 3:1), they began to change the Corinthians' understanding of what the *role* of the Christian apostle should be. Not only did they speak well, but they were capable of eliciting a wide range of pneumatic activity, such as healing, ecstatic utterances, and visions. These "signs" lent authenticity to their claim that they were the true apostles and should be granted the right to exercise their authority in the Corinthian church.

Paul's understanding of apostolic ministry was displaced and he was forced into the orbit of these charismatic figures, trying to find some way to respond. Second Corinthians 10-13 is part of a letter which reveals that Paul *refused* to be identified by the same social and theological criteria as these interlopers (2 Cor. 10:18). In fact, the letter was a form of discourse that allowed Paul to distance himself from the conflict. From this critical distance, Paul was able to change the Corinthians' notion of what it meant to be a "true" apostle—it was not evidence of ecstatic power, but identification with Jesus Christ. Had Paul tried to conform to the accepted concept of the apostolic role that had taken root at Corinth, he would not have been empowered to speak the truth, not only of his own personhood, but that of the Gospel. Indeed, Paul changed the reigning notion of discipleship by being honest with himself before God and the Corinthian church and by finding a creative way to respond. The Spirit of Christ was not necessarily revealed in powerful expressions of miraculous activity but was rather evident in one's "weakness."

Although we are indebted to Paul for many things in this encounter, I want to highlight one thing in particular. At Corinth, Paul was able to establish distance from the notions of apostolic leadership that dominated the early Christian movement by exercising his own strengths as a communicator and by enacting a new dimension of Christian character. He did this by creating a persona that, when made present as an embodied voice in the community, established Paul's legitimacy as an authentic spokesperson for Christ. The persona of Paul's letter reflected more of Paul's character than the Corinthians had seen. The "voice" or personal presence which was speaking in the letter was Paul *but it was also not Paul*. Paul-in-the-letter made the listener more aware of the personhood or ethos of Paul and that pointed to the personhood of Jesus Christ.

Like the church at Corinth, the contemporary Christian church has looked to the culture for "social characters" that shape our notion of leadership.

> Following the general pattern of bureaucratization, the churches, too, have focused on routinized problem solving in the organization and maintenance of their institutions as the chief locus of the leadership effectiveness. In other words, the minister as Manager is

the strongest candidate for the dominant image of professional leadership. [12]

When the Manager steps onto the stage of our social relations, we expect a certain kind of behavior. We expect this character to help us identify and then solve our institutional problems, or, by adopting the role of therapist, help us solve our personal problems as well. Since our managerial culture's highest value is organization and structure, we expect our leaders to speak in the ways my seminary student spoke—with a high premium on organizing information, the architecture of ideas, technique and form, but little emphasis on shaping experience.

As Aristotle cautioned speakers in a much earlier age, too much emphasis on technique overlooks ethos: the persuasive aspects of our own characters. The problem for us is similar to Paul's. How do we find the distance between our own character and the dominant social characters of our age? "Managers" at least tell us how to organize information, solve institutional and personal problems, and become proficient at applying scientific theory to a given situation. But as my seminary student experienced and as our friend, the English teacher, observed, when we try to manage our impressions within the role of "professional," we may lose our own sense of who we are. Moreover, our listeners are desperately looking for something new in professional church leadership, and therefore, in their experience of preaching. Hough and Cobb note:

> Although it is true that professional church leaders must be good at organizational development and maintenance, the modern idea of the professional manager, as one who solves problems by the application of scientific theory, is simply not adequate as an image for church leadership. [13]

The ministerial student discovered at his speech assessment that his own voice was inhibited by the managerial persona. He realized that he needed permission from his community of hearers to recover his own witness to the Gospel. His sermon would reveal more of the truth of who he was only when he made connections between his experience and the tradition of faith, thereby creating fresh interpretations for his listeners. Only then does the preacher's persona, a voice and presence which is you—and more than you—when you preach, resonate with the truth of experience.

COMMUNICATION AS PERFORMANCE

Models of communication which emphasize the shape of the message at the expense of the speaker make it more difficult to understand the oral dynamics of the act of preaching. There are some other, more promising, trajectories in the study of rhetoric which have originated in Aristotle's discussion of ethos. References to the character of the speaker bring to mind a rich storehouse of images in the rhetorical tradition. Perhaps the most luminous association comes from a scene in Shakespeare's *As You Like It*. In Act 2, scene 7, Jacques speaks the speech that has become a seminal metaphor for all human social behavior: "All the world's a stage, and all the men and women merely players: they have their exits and their entrances; and one man in his time plays many parts."

Most preachers will recognize in their experience the truth of Shakespeare's dictum that "all the world's a stage" upon which they are expected to "play many parts": preacher, pastoral counselor, parent, spouse, or friend. In the midst of this fragmentation of time and self, ministers grope for any unifying construct that gives congruity and coherence to their self-understanding and presentation, particularly in the space between pulpit and pew.

Shakespeare demonstrated that images of theatricality can open up fresh perceptions of who we are and how we interpret ourselves to each other and to ourselves. We speak easily of roles that we play in the various arenas of our lives and struggle between audiences who compete for our concentration, time, and energy. Those who study social behavior have long used the metaphor of life as theater to understand how cultures and individuals within those cultures communicate and how coherence and cohesiveness are established within communities. A "performance perspective" is emerging in other disciplines of communication and would be very promising to the study of preaching. It would emphasize effectiveness, that is, how congruity between the voice of the preacher, the persona which emerges in the sermon, and the deep inner voice which calls the community to discipleship *creates* and *generates* faithful response within the preacher and within those communities which hear the spoken sermon.

The first step in opening up a performance perspective in the study of preaching is to redeem the term "performance." All of us have had those quiet conversations in the hallways of the church where someone suggested: "Isn't preaching a lot like *acting*, Reverend?" Admit it, you would squirm when they said that. Some even believed that the theater or a drama class in college was a good place to learn to preach. But you did not want to be "an actor" in the pulpit, did you? Like most others, you make pejorative associations when the discussion turns to "performance" in the pulpit.

You come by that reaction honestly. Jonas Barish notes that our language betrays our prejudice against "performance." When we wish to praise some aspect of human behavior, we often borrow metaphors from the arts: the woman's voice was so "musical" when she spoke, his struggle with the board members was "epic," the preacher's description of the episode was so "graphic" that it compelled us to listen, or her garden was "sculpturesque."

Yet if we wish to demean someone or something, we have a bag full of epithets that we can take from the theater: she is so "melodramatic," that church is too "theatrical" and the preacher "stagey," don't pay any attention to her—she is just "playacting," or I was embarrassed when that couple "made a scene" in the restaurant.[14] Everyday life, we say, is not the place for a performance, never mind the pulpit! It is taken to be a sham or a form of pretense.

This is not the way the term is being used in virtually all other studies in human communication. The performance perspective is built upon the view that humankind is *homo histrio*, that is, "a definition of human beings as essentially performing creatures who constitute and sustain their identities and collectively enact their worlds through roles and rituals."[15] Do we not as Christians understand liturgy to be the ritual by which we understand our Christian identity? Are we so far away from talking about worship as performance? What then of preaching as a central act of worship? How does our own performance within the context of worship give definition to other "enactments" or "roles" that are expected of us in our communities?

The term *performance* comes from the old French *par + fournir* which literally means to "carry through to completion."[16] This more positive association makes it possible to rehabilitate the use of this term in our discussion of truthful communication in the pulpit. What is it that we do when we speak the sermon we have written in the study? Do we not bring it forth to completion in the act of speaking it? Does the form of sermon "come through" our bodies, our voices, our selves? Preaching is a performance of the sermon, that is, a vocal and physical action through which the form of the sermon becomes sound and image. The sermon becomes transformed from something which is encoded in print on a page into an oral-aural event for both preacher and hearer.

Clyde Fant has effectively demonstrated that the goal of preaching is the creation of an oral-aural (and I might add, a visual) experience and not the production of a literary, written sermon.[17] Within this sensory experience of the sermon, both the preacher and listener understand what is "real," what is truthful, immutable, and the basis for Christian belief. Don Wardlaw discusses the goal of *preaching* the sermon as "the embodiment of the reality" presented in the sermon. *To embody* means "to incorporate," "to assimilate," or "to identify with." Embodied delivery, then, "shows a high degree of coherence between what the preacher says and how he or she says it."[18]

The performance perspective on preaching builds upon these concepts of sermon as oral event and speaking the sermon as embodied delivery and, as such, helps us understand the *end* of preaching. How does it help us understand the *means?* There is another clue from the etymology of "performance." Literally, per/formance means "form coming through."[19] Actors, oral interpreters, storytellers, and others who have an experiential understanding of performance processes perceive, for example, that when an oral interpreter reads a poem aloud to an audience, the *form* of the poem comes through the speaker. When a storyteller tells a story, he or she allows the *form* of the story to "come through'' in the telling. In the enactment of a play, the form of a character comes through the actor playing the role. Similarly, when you preach, the form of your sermon either comes through or does not come through your character, your body, your voice, the ''individual, private miracle'' that is your self *and* the part of you that is formed by the community.

A sermon's form consists of voices, images, ideas, and interpretations woven into some definitive design for speaking. In preparing to preach a sermon, the minister must find points of connection with those elements of the sermon design if it is to ''come through.'' It is this characteristic of the sermon-in-performance that makes it truthful: the rhetorical form of discourse which is identified by the church as sermon must come through the character (ethos) of the preacher. Let us take a look at how this perspective began to take root in one preacher's experience.

A PARABLE OF PREACHING PERFORMANCE

Andrew was noted for his skill in preaching. In fact, he was sought after by other pastors to preach revival meetings. By most standards, Andrew was an effective preacher. His church was a new congregation and was rapidly adding members and constructing new facilities every year. Most of Andrew's peers considered Andrew to be a premier preacher in their conference.

Andrew became a part of a preaching peer group that was going to work at making their preaching more effective. They would look together at new methods of sermon preparation and biblical study, but they were particularly interested in experimenting with new ways of delivering sermons that would improve their interaction with listeners *outside* the boundaries of the established church.

The first event they planned together was a communication effectiveness seminar that put them into the same learning group with nonpreachers such as business executives, government officials, corporate vice-presidents, and teachers. The methods offered in the seminar challenged Andrew's notions about how to preach. When Andrew had been in seminary, he was often evaluated on what he said in the sermon but never on how he spoke.

He was taught techniques for designing the message. It would be the message that would speak, not Andrew. To deliver a message, one only had to speak clearly and loudly.

In this seminar, Andrew was taking a look at who he was *in the act of speaking* for the first time. There was no time to prepare a complex message. One had to speak extemporaneously about something the speaker felt strongly about. These exercises were videotaped for review. When Andrew looked at himself on videotape, he saw that he was stiff, stilted, frustrated, and according to the other nonpreachers in the seminar, he looked and sounded "like a preacher." When he tried the simple suggestions of the seminar leader to relax his body and voice, he was unsuccessful. He felt defensive, guarded, and afraid to be vulnerable. He was definitely not available to the suggestions of this audience *or to the promptings of his own inner voice.*

Andrew realized that he was trapped in a role that did not permit him much freedom of expression. He saw for himself that very little of who he was was coming through in his speaking. If that was the case, how much of the Gospel of Jesus Christ ever came through in his body and voice? He had become successful at mastering a set of techniques that his community had identified as normal for effective preaching. Yet these normalities were restricting the ways people could hear and that he could speak. A lot of who he was was missing in his presentation. How could he speak in a way that made him a credible witness of the Gospel to those *outside* that community who thought he "looked and sounded like a preacher?"

When Andrew went back to his room that night, he was despondent and discouraged. He did not feel that the methods which had made him effective in one setting were serving him well in this one. In fact, he was tense and angry and this tension was revealing itself in his body and voice. His voice was pinched, his throat was sore, and his upper body was tight and constricted. Why was he not able to "let go" and make himself more available to his listeners and to his subject matter? He struggled with whether or not to leave the seminar and go back to what was familiar to him. The assignment he had been given for the next day's session was to give a talk in which he had to "level" with his listeners about something meaningful in his experience. He was not sure he could do that. Why did he feel that he could not communicate his feeling of frustration and despair to this group of listeners? And if he did not feel that he could do this simple exercise on this occasion, how could he "level" with his listeners about the meaning of the Gospel each week in the pulpit?

Andrew went out to eat at a favorite restaurant with a friend that night. The place held many good memories for Andrew. On one occasion he had brought his own daughter here and talked with her about the importance of marriage and how meaningful a commitment it would be when she was ready to make it. "Marriage is a total gift of self," he had said to her, "and is made out of love, faith and trust." That night he had offered her a gift of a cross on a gold chain to remind her of his own parental love for her.

Suddenly, a light went on for Andrew. What was preaching but a kind of marriage between speaker and listener? Did not the Christian preacher embody a story of God's self-giving? Does not the Gospel prompt us to risk that kind of giving when we speak? We trust our listeners because we trust the Spirit of God. It is not the level of our skill, personality, or ability that makes the Gospel come through for listeners or preachers alike. It is a gift of grace. That belief gives us the basis for trusting ourselves. Was not this task of preaching the Good News actually a gift that God had given to Andrew in the same way Andrew had given a gift to his daughter? There was no reason to withhold himself any longer.

Andrew remembered performing the marriage ceremony for his daughter and son-in-law some months before. In that ceremony, she wore that same cross and gold chain. The memory brought tears to Andrew's eyes. With this memory came the discovery of what he would say to the other seminar members.

The next day, Andrew "leveled" with his listeners. He told them about his anger and frustration the day before. Then he retold of the experience the memory in the restaurant had brought forth. He did not need to interpret this experience to his listeners. They realized and shared in this experience of the Gospel by observing what had happened to him physically and vocally. Andrew had become more fully available to his own message. The tension in his upper body was gone, his voice was not constricted or pinched, his face was not set in a frowning mask, and he was carefully establishing eye contact with them.

Instead of being an accomplished but frustrated speaker, Andrew had now become a powerful witness to the emergent and spontaneous power of the Gospel. His listeners were trusting him now because of the reality coming through his body, voice, and character. Andrew had risked being honest with his listeners, sharing the intersection between the Gospel and his own inner life. He was not intellectualizing now, but speaking from his own experience. In the oral and written feedback that Andrew received from the group, each one affirmed that Andrew was on a journey toward a different speaking style, one that would make himself and his own experience available to his listeners, one that would make fuller and freer use of his voice and body as vehicles for the sermon, and one that would establish greater rapport with his listeners.

The challenge for Andrew was to translate this experience into a way of making some different choices for speaking all of his sermons. In a series of "before and after" videotapes in a follow-up seminar, Andrew started to see the changes taking place in his preaching style. He could see that his face, upper body, and voice were very different indeed. The stern and furrowed countenance was becoming more animated. He was *seeing* his listeners and his hands and arms were sculpting more of what he was seeing in his sermon when he spoke. Andrew was finding that he was spending more time filling out concrete images in his sermons rather than building complex outlines. He admitted that he was certainly enjoying himself more as he spoke. Because more of the sermon was coming through him, he was getting more energy for speaking from it. His voice was losing its predictable rhythms and vocal patterns as he punctuated his speech with more pauses and shorter sentences. Andrew did not need to be taught the techniques of good speech as much as he needed to be released to do what came naturally.

As he looked at the tapes, Andrew realized he had a long way to go. The most important point was, he saw that he was becoming more effective. He was "per/forming" the sermon now, that is, allowing himself to be an instrument for the emotional, intellectual, and sensual aspects of his sermon to come through to completion. The look and sound of his preaching was changing. Andrew was seeing for himself that the person who was speaking the sermon on the videotape was more fully him. However, he realized that it was also *not* him. The persona of Andrew-in-the-sermon was more like but also more *unlike* Andrew himself. That was the truth coming through for him in the sermon: the one who is performing the sermon is me but is also *not me*.

THE HOMILETICAL AND THEOLOGICAL GROUND OF THE PERFORMANCE PERSPECTIVE

Lest we think that a performance perspective is foreign to homiletics, let us review some basic principles advanced by forebears in the tradition. Dietrich Bonhoeffer was one who struggled to identify what the rhetorical ends and means of preaching were. But perhaps one of the most stimulating issues he addressed was this question of form.

> The form of the preached word is different from every other form of speech. Other speeches are structured so that they have some truth which they wish to communicate either behind them or beneath them or over them, or else they are arranged so as to express an emotion or teach a concept. These human words communicate something else besides what they are of themselves. They become means to an end. The meaning of the proclaimed word, however, does not lie outside of itself; it is the thing itself . . . the historical Jesus Christ, who bears humanity upon himself with all of its sorrows and its guilt. The sustaining Christ is the dimension of the preached word.[20]

For Bonhoeffer, the stakes of preaching were high. He hoped for no less than the emergence of "the historical Jesus Christ" in the preaching event. Our role is to speak in ways that do not hinder or obstruct the form of the active, sustaining Presence of Christ as it moves through the congregation.

If the form of the sermon is the Word, what it comes through is the character of the preacher. Phillips Brooks, emphasizing this emergent quality of truth in preaching, said that "the truth must *come really through the person* [emphasis mine]," not merely over his or her lips, not merely into a person's understanding and out through his or her pen. "It must come through his character, [her] affections, his whole intellectual and moral being. It must come genuinely through [the preacher]."[21]

Brooks employs two theatrical metaphors to distinguish between two kinds of reality in preaching:

> There is the first ground of the vicious habit that our congregations have of talking about the preacher more than they think about the truth. The minstrel who sings before you to show his skill, will be praised for his wit, and rhymes, and voice. But the courier who hurries in, breathless, to bring you a message, will be forgotten in the message that he brings.[22]

Brooks identifies a basic tension in sermon performance. We all know of sermons that are preached in ways that reveal more the characteristics of the preacher, rather than her or his character. It is interesting that we may speak of these preachers pejoratively as "performers" because very little of the Word's form is "coming through" in preaching. In her book *SpeakEasy*, speech consultant Sandy Linver identifies a "performer" as the type of speaker who

> focuses on the speaker, at the expense of the audience and the message. He (the speaker) impresses people at first as an accomplished speaker: He brims with self-confidence, has plenty of energy, speaks with a full, strong voice, is in command of his subject matter, seems perfectly at ease, and is the kind of person envied by others as a "natural" speaker. But as much as his audience admires his style and envies his poise, they find it hard to listen to him—although they may be hard put to say exactly why.[23]

By contrast, Brooks uses performance imagery to describe a congruity between speaker and message. He refers to a "courier, who hurries in, breathless." More than a bearer of a message, the courier is the very embodiment of an urgent word.

83

Brooks's description of truthful preaching can be compared to Alla Bozarth-Campbell's description of truthful performance. Brooks suggests that the truth of preaching has the same kind of emergent quality as the truth of a performed poem.[24] In *The Word's Body: An Incarnational Aesthetic of Interpretation*, Bozarth-Campbell develops an aesthetic of performance which is instructive to preachers. Her perspective as a Christian minister and theologian helps her understand the process by which a silent or oral reading of a poem becomes a "shared experience of communion." "Performance" is a term which describes the form of a text coming through the body and voice of the reader.[25] The poem then "becomes truly lived experience and is finally presented to the world in a transformed state. . . . This world may be the private world of a single reader alone in his or her chair, or it may be the public world of stage, church, auditorium, electronic media, or artist's chamber."[26] Similarly, for Brooks, the message that a preacher brings cannot be "true" until it "comes through" the experience of the preacher. Here is one of those rare places where performer and homiletician are on the same firm theological ground and invite some analogies within communication arts.

YOUR ROLE AS A CHRISTIAN PREACHER: ENGAGING THE VOICE DEEP WITHIN

Should some actor or actress be assigned to play the part of Brook's "courier with an urgent message," he or she would aspire to congruity in performance. Any actor or actress who called attention to him or herself and not to the substance of what he was saying would be severely reprimanded by any self-respecting director. Effective actors work diligently at being transparent to the characters they are playing. Storytellers become effective when the listener cannot determine where the art of the storyteller ends and the art of the story begins. Their hope is that they will so identify with narrator (or controlling perspective) in the story that an audience will experience the fullness of the story, not the characteristics of their art.

That is why the actor's or storyteller's art is so instructive to the preacher. To achieve the desired quality of transparency, the actor and storyteller must find points of identification between his or her experience and the fictive experience of the characters. Preachers, actors, oral intepreters, or storytellers who stand "outside" of what they are saying will speak with detachment, artificiality, or disassociation. Ironically, this incongruity between speaker and speech is what the listener often refers to pejoratively as "performance." As witnesses to the Incarnation, we need to reclaim this fundamental metaphor for describing processes of preaching. The primary task of speaking the sermon is to allow the form of the Word to come through us, not call attention to our characteristic ways of speaking. The Voice "deep within" us which "calls us to do what is right" and which "comes through" in the performance of a sermon is that of the Risen Christ.

A performance perspective helps us reclaim some basic rhetorical and theological principles for speaking a sermon.

1. It emphasizes how the form of the sermon does or does not come through the character of the one speaking.

2. It establishes congruity between one's voice and presence for speaking and the deep and inner voices that arise from our private and communal selves.

3. It helps us identify the boundaries between our role as preacher and other enactments of self within and outside our communities of faith.

4. The performance perspective stresses the distance between the person-who-speaks and the persona of the sermon and therefore frees us from the dominance of "social characters" that shape our notions of effectiveness.

Ken Burns, the producer of the acclaimed series on the Civil War for public television wrote:

> Much like Gutenberg, half a millennia ago, we are poised to embrace new ways of speaking to one another . . . a whole new literature, a poetry for the eye as well as the ear . . . we must begin to trust the language of these new forms. Better yet we must study them.[27]

By accentuating the oral-aural-visual dimensions of the act of preaching, the performance perspective studies the ways we use our physical selves in speaking the sermon. It points to new ways of speaking to one another. The metaphor of "performance" helps us understand that the sermon can be "poetry for the eye as well as the ear." The following exercises are designed to help you embrace a new way of speaking by establishing greater congruity between your personhood and your speaking persona.

EXERCISES

1. Have someone record a candid, everyday conversation you have in the performance of your professional role. Note the patterns of inflection in your voice, the rhythm and pace of your speech, and other characteristics of your speaking voice. Identify what you like and be able to record this in a journal or share it with your preaching peer group.

2. Now listen to your voice as you preach a sermon. Do you note any variation of pitch, inflection, or quality from your other "voice"? Try to read your sermon aloud in your "natural" voice and record that. Work for greater congruity between your preaching persona and your natural speech.

3. Recall the sound of a preacher who exerted a great deal of influence upon you. Can you identify any physical or vocal mannerisms that you might have picked up from your mentor?

4. Watch a preacher on television or listen to another in the pulpit. Be as descriptive as you can about his or her "performance." Of the four qualities listed here, which seems to dominate the speaker's attention?

   a. performer (preacher)
   b. text
   c. event (or awareness of the context of preaching event)
   d. audience awareness

Note what your reaction to the preacher is. What does the actual event of preaching evoke from you? Assign adjectives to describe the *persona* of the preacher you are watching or listening to. What gestures, sounds, or words elicit these descriptive phrases from you? (For example, if you say "trustworthy," what aspects of the performed sermon create that impression?)

5. In *Learning Preaching*, Don Wardlaw describes how video-taping can be used as a resource for learning to preach.[28] He suggests that the goal of preaching a sermon is "embodied delivery," that is, the way the meaning of the sermon "comes through" the preacher's body and voice. These moments of connection and congruity between the preacher and the persona of the sermon can be seen on video camera.

Arrange for a videotaping session for your preaching group. Plan a sermon or sermon excerpt that you will present to this group. Discuss the following concepts and questions drawn from Wardlaw's work:

- Where did you feel most connected to your sermon as you preached it? Where did you feel most disconnected?
- Locate, if you can, these places on the tape. "Exegete" these images. What message(s) are you transmitting?
- Now block out the picture. Listen to your voice. What impressions do you receive from simply listening to yourself?
- Speed the images forward and watch what physical patterns are repeated in your movements. What impressions do you receive when watching these patterns of movement?
- Videotape an impromptu exercise in which you speak without notes on what you take your "gospel" to be. Compare the images presented here from those when you are preaching. Which parts of your natural self emerge and how can you identify them physically and vocally?
- Discuss the changes you would like to make in your preaching style.

Chapter 5

Listening to the Biblical Text

The reading of Scriptures must seem to come from a deep realization of the Infinite.

—S. S. Curry

Preaching is one oral event that usually follows another: the public presentation of scripture by the preacher or by someone else in the worshiping community. The preacher has probably prepared for these oral events by reading and reflecting in silence, paying little attention to the oral values of the text before him. Even though the end of reading the text and preaching the sermon is "oral," the process of preparing for the reading of the text and speaking the sermon "is envisioned as outside the world of voice."[1] In this chapter we will explore the dynamics of the oral-aural world that the biblical text came from and to which the text and sermon will return. Understanding this world will help you read the text aloud as preparation for developing and preaching your sermon.

THE PREACHER AS LISTENER

In seminary, there was much discussion about the world the text came from, the politics which made its production necessary, and even the rhetorical features of its form. The ministerial student was encouraged to hone her writing skills, and she produced papers that revealed abstract meanings and ideas about the text. These were all valuable forms of learning and deepened the preacher's awareness of the uniqueness of each piece of sacred scripture. However, there was never much attempt to explore a basic feature of these texts.

Biblical texts originated in the world of sound and were recorded so that they might be spoken! They are a collection of stories to be told, letters to be read aloud, prophetic words to be uttered, proscriptions for behavior to be announced, psalms and hymns to be sung, and sermons to be preached. It is strange that we have become so accustomed to thinking in visual and spatial categories that we have overlooked this basic orientation of biblical revelation.

Examine the scriptures for references to the voice and ear and you will understand that these texts were written so that they might be more faithfully returned to acoustical space. Seminarians even now rarely have the chance to listen to texts voiced in ways that stimulate the imagination. When the text is read aloud, in worship or in study groups, the reader often accentuates the distance that exists between voice and text, as if to suggest that voicing the text would lend little to the discussion of meaning. The seminarian has usually been coached to listen only for its theological content and is rewarded for clever assessments of the ideas presented in the readings. Very little attention is devoted to the text's oral values or to the experience of listening to the text being read aloud. Walter Ong notes that this is a curious way to study these and indeed any text:

> Despite the oral roots of all verbalization, the scientific and literary study of language and literature has for centuries until quite recent years, shied away from orality. Texts have clamored for attention so peremptorily that oral creations have tended to be regarded generally as variants of written productions or, if not this, beneath serious scholarly attention. Only recently have we become impatient with our obtuseness here.[2]

Preachers can feel listeners beginning to push against the obtuseness that Ong is referring to. Listeners live in a media world where information is imparted by speakers whose electronically transmitted bodies and voices energize scripts or texts and catch the listeners' attention. Yet when a listener enters a place of worship, information is transmitted to her or him by speakers who seem emotionally detached from what they are saying. When they do arrive in the listeners' world of sound, the texts have been divested of their oral values. They sound lifeless, uninteresting, and irrelevant when read aloud. Listeners are forced to await the preacher's explanation of the ideas present in the text to understand its claim to authority. To alleviate this objectifying approach, we can treat texts as voices which belong to the world of sound:

> Here instead of reducing words to objects, urns, or even icons, we take them simply as what they are even more basically, as utterances, that is to say, as cries. All verbalization, including all literature, is radically a cry, a sound emitted from the interior of a person.[3]

Reading texts aloud gives the listener access to the interiority of the persons who recorded that text. When we lend our voices to the task of interpretation, we begin to treat the text as human utterance rather than abstract object. The preacher has the opportunity to listen to these cries that have come across time, but only if she dares to return them to acoustical space. Listeners not only make better preachers of sermons, but better public readers of texts.

THE PREACHER'S ROLE AS ORAL READER OF THE TEXT

It is puzzling that most preachers do not pay more attention to the public reading of the very texts they have spent a long time studying in silence. When a preacher enters the pulpit to preach a sermon on a text or selection of texts, she brings with her a personal relationship with that text. Not only has the preacher studied the background of these texts, but she has asked it questions, wrestled with it, tried to walk away from it, argued with it, and finally (if she is lucky) received the gift of insight from it. Yet when the preacher reads it aloud to the congregation, she usually treats it as an "object" from which she is detached.

Why does the preacher refuse to lend to the text the gifts of his or her personality in rendering it to others? Why does the preacher withhold the music of his voice, the gentle gesture of the body, or the emotional richness of his conviction when the text is presented to listeners? Most people in our world do not make a habit of silently reading the Bible. In a recent survey conducted by the Barna Research Group of Glendale, California, the researchers found a high degree of "biblical illiteracy" among American adults, Christians and non-Christians alike.

> Many Christians do not even know things such as where Jesus was born or what the Bible contains . . . If they are uninformed about elementary things such as these, how can they be expected to intelligently discuss the content of the Scriptures with an unbeliever or to live in a manner consistent with biblical principles?[4]

If people are not reading their Bibles in silence at home, then their only experiences of Scripture are the oral renditions the preacher or lector offers in worship. Why do preachers and lectors fail to take this responsibility more seriously?

Preachers in our age come by it honestly. There has not been much encouragement to think about the listeners' aural experience of the text. As a result of this neglect, preachers have developed a poor reputation as public readers. Even Mark Twain noted:

> The church is always trying to get other people to reform; it might not be a bad idea to reform itself a little, by way of example. . . . The average clergyman could not fire into his congregation with a shotgun and hit a worse reader than himself, unless that weapon scattered shamefully. I am not meaning to be flippant and irreverent, I am only meaning to be truthful. The average clergyman, in all countries and of all denominations, is a very bad reader.[5]

In 1903, a speech teacher named S. S. Curry wrote *Vocal and Literary Interpretation of the Bible* to respond to a crisis in the professional ministry—the poor oral readings of platform speakers in the worship services. He begins the book by asking a question:

"Who has not felt dissatisfaction with the way the Bible is read in public?" We have heard resonances of that question even to our day. Curry devised a method which would restore the literature of the Bible to an oral milieu by way of "vocal expression" of the Bible in worship. He believed that effective public readings of the Scripture would enhance the meaning and experience of Scripture for both the reader and the audience. "The reading of Scriptures," he says, "must seem to come from a deep realization of the Infinite."[6]

Apparently, this "deep realization of the Infinite" is still not the goal of most public readers of Scripture. In fact, one of my students told me of the following suggestion one of his parishioners had: a woman stopped him after worship one Sunday. The look on her face suggested she was very excited about something. "I have a wonderful idea I want to share with you!" she exclaimed. "I know how we can cut out 10 minutes in worship every Sunday!" The pastor was naturally curious and anxious to hear her idea and was quick to tell her so. "We could just do away with reading the Scripture!" she said.[7] Just as preachers have not yet learned to tune their ears to the voices and cries of Scripture, so have their people not been encouraged to listen imaginatively. If we are to change our ways of listening and reading aloud, we must change our habits of thought about the way Scripture should be rendered orally in worship. "Thought itself relates in an altogether special way to sound."[8]

RECITATION OR PERFORMANCE?

Most preachers balk at the task of becoming better public readers or even encouraging skillful readers in their congregations to become lectors. There continues to be a deep-seated ambivalence about "performing" or "dramatizing" the Scripture in worship. The assumption is that one who gives an oral interpretation by employing voice and body in the presentation of the text is "acting," inappropriately calling attention to one's own gifts of expression in a house of worship. Or, those who do not mind this sort of expression in presenting texts believe that it necessitates special skills or knowledge that they themselves do not have and so they do not make *any* move toward enlivening the Word. These are honest concerns that deserve careful treatment.

Both the impulse to orally enliven Scripture and the impulse to restrain (even suppress) this type of expression are rooted in the church's tradition of recitation. Jonas Barish, as noted in the previous chapter, has shown that our language betrays our prejudice against "performance." Everyday life is not the place for a performance; it is taken to be a sham or a form of pretense rather than something authentic or truthful. When Thespis first stepped out from a Greek chorus and played a role, he was called a liar by one of his contemporaries because he was pretending to be someone else.[9] Those who continue that ancient practice give performances in the rarefied atmosphere of the stage or concert hall where lights and scenery help to sustain illusions and fictions. Those who purchase their tickets enter this space and appreciate the skill with which the performers sustain these illusions of being someone or somewhere else. Hopefully, they will leave that place with some sense of the "truthfulness" of artistic representation.

Church, we assume, is a different kind of space. It is designated for prayer and the worship of God. Except in the case of an occasional concert or chancel drama, the worshiper would not borrow from the language of the theater to describe his or her experience in church. Christian worshipers enter these spaces expecting to hear immutable truths presented about the Oneness of God, not the ephemeral "truths" sustained by skillful presentations of dramatized fictions. What happens in church is "real" to the Christian; what happens in the performance space is truthful, but still "unreal."[10]

We have inherited this deeply ingrained suspicion about performance from Plato and, in the Christian tradition, from Augustine. Plato considered such forms of "imitation" as "acting" and "reciting" deceptive, dangerous, and therefore corrupting. Augustine saw in theatrical display the manifestation of the devil and false gods.[11] Small wonder, then, why preachers are hesitant to change their thinking about performance in the pulpit or even at the lectern.

The prejudice against dramatics and performance has reduced

the significance of the public reader's role in worship. The lector is discouraged from using his or her voice or body in ways that enliven the listener's experience of hearing the text because of its association with playacting. Ideally, the reader is supposed to maintain a critical detachment from the text and orally present it with a minimum of personal engagement. There is little for the reader to do except speak clearly, and not many of them do that. As a consequence, the congregation of listeners invest very little of themselves in the act of listening. They certainly do not expect the reading of the text to make much of an impact on their ongoing experience of worship.

These conventions which govern the speaking and reading of texts in worship were developed in and for a different world than the one we now live in. When I was taught to read, I was encouraged to depart from the practice of my ancestors when they read, that is, I was taught *not* to move my lips as my eyes came across the words on a page. In fact, I was embarrassed when my grandmother would use her finger to keep her place when she read and mutter as her eyes caught the words. It was considered bad manners when your "reading" disturbed someone else's concentration. "Good" reading was reading in silence and solitude.

There was an entire program in my denomination that encouraged the practice of spiritual growth through daily Bible readings. When I came to church on Sunday mornings, my Sunday school teacher would ask: "How many of you did your daily Bible readings this week?" We would raise our hands or in some cases lift our Bibles to show that we had indeed read significant portions of our Bibles to ourselves in silence throughout the week. We were given a rather thin guidebook which took us through a week of readings and then asked us pertinent questions on what we read. This was an effective way to internalize Scripture and become aware of the basic theological ideas presented there. Silent reading allowed me to decode the signs printed on the pages of the Bible and translate them into Word. Still, I thought of the words as sounds and was often encouraged to take the next step: memorizing the verses. "Scripture memory" was understood to be a discipline by which one could resist temptation by hiding God's Word in one's heart. In the community of faith that nurtured me as a child, silent reading and scripture memory were the basis for personal, spiritual formation. Reading in silence was the skill necessary for a primary experience of the biblical stories. Once one acquired that skill, one acquired access to the spiritual resources available in the church and became conversant with theological ideas.

Since our faith community was so dependent on this process, there was little need for public reading when we met together. Reading aloud was only a pretext to the topic of the Sunday school lesson, the Bible study, or the presentation of the sermon. The goal was to make the scriptures "live" by discussing the *ideas* which were lifted from the text and determining how to apply them to our lives. We even explored other texts where these same ideas appeared. We certainly did not take much time to read the texts themselves aloud to each other. There did not seem to be inherent value in that activity. In fact, when we were given long passages to read aloud in a class meeting, we complained about their length, read them reluctantly, and hoped someone else would quickly be appointed to relieve us when we got tired of the assigned chore. *Listening* to these passages being read was no less difficult!

In worship, we were encouraged to "follow along in our Bibles" as someone (usually the preacher) read the passage he or she was to preach on. The focus of our attention was on the text being read, not upon the *reading* of the text, and upon the sermon which was to follow. Of course we sang the texts of the Bible as psalms and hymns and spoke them antiphonally as responsive readings in worship, but the act of reading the scripture aloud by someone in our community in worship was informal and perfunctory. It was deemed inappropriate for someone to read these texts with any kind of feeling because that person would have distracted our attention from the text. The structures of our congregational life were developed within and for this culture of silent print, a culture that prized the skill of silent reading as a way to experience a personal relationship with God and prepare for communal study of the ideas found in the biblical text. "Memory work" was a deeper engagement with those ideas as strategies for living, and feelings were inappropriate resources for presenting the texts in worship.

Now we find ourselves confronted with the task of communicating in a different media world. Electronic culture has its own norms and values for communicating the Gospel. Walter Ong points out that no media age completely displaces the values of the age that precedes it. It does however intensify and build upon those values in developing norms for "good" communication.

The most dramatic shift between the silent print and electronic culture is in what happens to texts. Ong points out in *Orality and Literacy: The Technologizing of the Word* that "the electronic age is . . . . an age of 'secondary orality,' the orality of telephones, radio, and television, which depends on writing and print for its existence."[12] The newscaster or politician uses a teleprompter or teletype machine in making a report or speech on television. However, the speaker does not call attention to the text he or she is using. In fact, the audience may never be aware of that text because that audience member is concentrating on the speaker. That speaker or reporter concentrates on making eye contact with the audience by looking at the camera.

Those who are effective speakers on television are adept at making the audience feel as if that speaker is talking directly to them and including them when she or he speaks. Select anyone you feel is effective on television and consider *why* he or she is effective. Observe what happens to printed matter. Texts are scripts for oral discourse. You are drawn quickly into the heart of that message when the speaker contacts you—through the speaker's eyes and by personal address. The text becomes the vehicle for, not the obstacle to, the speaker's message. There is no time for long, artful preface. Words are selected for your ears, not for your eyes. They are short, easy to retain, and vivid.

How can preachers learn from the electronic culture without sacrificing integrity? Many preachers want to enliven their oral presentation of Scripture. Some belong to a generation who have listened as the impact of biblical texts has been dulled by lifeless, detached readings. Others have had no meaningful experience of the biblical texts at all; they are discovering the Scriptures as if for the first time. This group of preachers wants to learn to translate their primary experience of the text with their voices and bodies, even as they work to create sermon designs that are appropriate to the rhetorical features of the biblical texts. At the same time, they do not want to call attention to their own style; they want to respect the distance between themselves and the text and thereby create adequate space for the listener to meet it for themselves.

The question for all of us is: how do we find ways of speaking and reciting that respect the norms and values of electronic culture without capitulating to its excesses? The culture that surrounds the electronic church has developed a "star" system. Authority comes from an individual's celebrity status in this subculture. There is a great temptation for preachers to imitate the styles and manners of these stars in order to hold an audience. How do we present our texts in a livelier manner without becoming "phony"? How do we reappropriate the resources of the culture of silent print to our electronic age?

The first thing for us to recognize is the value of recovering our own tradition of recitation. The church has lived through media transitions before and has always found ways of effectively communicating the Gospel. On any given Sunday in Christian churches throughout the world, scripture passages are being recited in a variety of ways. They are chanted in some places; in others they are recast as folk sermons. Some preachers are reading texts aloud informally from pulpit Bibles, others are telling the biblical stories *as* stories in worship. All presentations reflect, in some way, our own history of recitation.

Styles have developed in response to the medium that was dominant in particular ages. In an oral culture (that is, a culture that had not developed the technology of writing), the style of speaking was emotional, passionate, and spontaneous. The Christian movement developed in a culture that was highly literate but retained aspects of orality in communicating its message. "Manuscript" cultures treated texts as recordings of oral discourse. Reading was translation of word to sound; silent reading was unthinkable. On formal occasions, such as worship in house church or synagogue, a sacred text might be chanted to express respect for the "otherness" of the discourse, that it belonged to the realm of the sacred rather than the ordinary. The invention of the printing press made texts more accessible to larger numbers of people. Anyone could become a reader and hence have access to the sacred story by acquiring a copy of the book or pamphlet in which it was printed. This is when public reading became more informal. People were encouraged to read for themselves. By the eighteenth century, more and more readers were doing so in solitude and silence. Public reading was almost a contradiction in terms. Emotional expression of a printed text belonged to the province of "acting" or "elocution" and required skill and practice.[13]

If we are to find appropriate forms of expression in our electronic culture, we must first learn to draw upon this history. I redefine the electronic church to mean more than that church which is televised. It means the church that reflects the values of electronic culture. In *this* church the scripture texts will be presented in a variety of forms: they will be recast as stories and dramatic monologues, biblical narratives will be told as stories, we will recover the art of chanting, and they will be recited both informally and antiphonally. The history of recitation is accumulative, that is, forms and styles of expression build upon antecedents in rhetorical history. Our tradition of recitation is rich with possibilities. If we are going to find a way to present our sacred stories, we must first become aware of those possibilities.

Next, we must become more aware of the importance of reading scripture aloud as an act of worship. Charlotte Lee in her book *Oral Reading of Scriptures* states: "The Bible, like all other great literature, must be read aloud to realize its full potential."[14] Lectors need to understand the nature of what they are doing and learn how to prepare for the occasion. In *Effective Speech Communication in Leading Worship*, Charles Bartow explains a basic principle for reading Scripture aloud:

> The reading of Scriptures needs to be understood as an act of interpretative-situational speech. To read a passage from the Bible correctly . . . one has to develop some understanding of it and how to express that understanding accurately. Then, too, one has to be sensitive to the physical and liturgical setting in which the expression takes place.[15]

A steady diet of informal, unprepared public reading from the pulpit by preachers or lectors will become a hindrance to, rather than an enhancement of, the worship experience. This means we will have to reconsider the role of the lector in worship. We need to find ways to identify those in our congregations who are gifted public readers and who would be willing to learn the basic principles of reading aloud. I have often wondered what would happen if we thought of the ministry of the lector as we think of the ministry of music. What would happen if the preacher arrived at church, realized that he or she needed someone to sing a solo as an act of corporate worship, then appointed someone to sing something at the appropriate time. Or worse, what if the preacher decided to sing it him or herself without any preparation or rehearsal. What a disaster for the worshiper!

The ministry of music has taught us that there are some in virtually every congregation who enjoy practicing and singing together in worship. There are a good many who enjoy preparing solos. In many places there is a full- or part-time staff member devoted exclusively to enlivening worship through the ministry of music. We can use the model of the music ministry to help us prepare for a renewed ministry of the lector. There will be a good number of those in your congregation who, with encouragement and direction, can contribute much to enlivening the presentation of the Word in worship.

At this writing I am a part of a congregation which has a team of men and women whose ministry is the oral preparation of texts for reading in worship. Members of this team often comment how much their experience of the scriptural texts has been enhanced by preparing to present them aloud in worship. There is not a single actor or dramatist in this team, but they are all discovering their own gifts and styles for oral presentation. It is a joy to see members of the congregation lean forward in anticipation of hearing the scriptures read well by these who have chosen to do so.

To reclaim the ministry of the lector is to recover a neglected part of our heritage as a church. The first act of Jesus' public ministry, according to the Gospel of Luke, was an act of public hearing:

When he came to Nazareth, where he had been brought up, he went to the synagogue on the sabbath day, as was his custom. He stood up to read, and the scroll of the prophet Isaiah was given to him. He unrolled the scroll and found the place where it was written, "The Spirit of the Lord is upon me, because he has anointed me to preach good news to the poor. He has sent me to proclaim release to the captives and recovering of sight to the blind, to let the oppressed go free, to proclaim the year of the Lord's favor."

And he rolled up the scroll, gave it back to the attendant, and sat down. The eyes of all in the synagogue were fixed on him. Then he began to say to them, "Today this scripture has been fulfilled in your hearing." All spoke well of him and were amazed at the gracious words that came from his mouth.

Luke 4:16-22a

Jesus' own life and ministry were shaped by the performance conventions reflected here. Services of worship in the synagogue of Jesus' day were organized around the oral presentation (in the form of a chant) and oral interpretation of the sacred texts. It was considered to be a great honor to be asked to read aloud as Jesus did in the synagogue where he worshiped as a youth.

More was demanded of the public reader in Jesus' day than is in ours. This story shows that Jesus was presented with a scroll, indicating that the sacred memory had been recorded in that form. Yet in order to read it with authority, Jesus would have had to *know* it well. Tom Boomershine notes that the ancient manuscripts or scrolls had no punctuation and no spacing. In Hebrew manuscripts, there is no marking of vowels. The text is only consonantal. In order to read it, it would be necessary to memorize the vowels and melody marks. In Greek, the vowels are present. However, punctuation is not. The oral reader must supply the divisions of words, sentences, and melodies from memory.[16] Jesus' own message or oral interpretation of this passage reflects that his insight on his own ministry came from a deeply internalized knowledge of this particular text. Here is a lesson for our own ministries. When the texts are interiorized or known by heart, they generate insight and inspiration. When presented well, according to the conventions of recitation of the day, they evoke specific responses from listeners. Before he got in trouble with them, Jesus' listeners "spoke well of him and were amazed at the gracious words that came from his mouth." Jesus prepared his listeners to hear the difficult word he would say to them by effectively reciting the text so that they could *experience* it for themselves.

The community of faith that formed in response to Jesus' ministry and memory followed the same pattern of organization as the synagogue. Reading among the early Christians was re-creation of the memories of Jesus and of Israel's experience of God, not simply the transmission of information. We can imagine that those who read were highly regarded and honored members of that community and took their responsibilities very seriously.

No one understood the importance of public reading any better than the Apostle Paul. There are several indications in the Pauline corpus which suggest that Paul expected that his letter would be read aloud in worship. To open and close his letter, Paul freely uses formulas taken from liturgical constructions, particularly those used in the Lord's Supper.[17] At the end of both First Thessalonians and Colossians, Paul specifically directs that the letters be read aloud to the gathered congregation. He writes these directions to the Thessalonians: "I solemnly command you by the Lord that this letter be read to all of them" (1 Thess. 5:27) and to the Colossians: "And when this letter has been read among you, have it read also in the church of the Laodiceans; and see that you read also the letter from Laodicea" (Col. 4:16).

In fact, Thomas Boomershine notes that in Judaism, reading in silence was forbidden. On one occasion, one rabbi adominished another: "O keen scholar, open your mouth and read (the written tradition), open your mouth and repeat (the oral tradition) so that (your knowledge) may be maintained in you and that which you have learned may live."[18] Public reading of the apostolic letter was aimed at building up the Body of Christ, consolidating the communal identity of the Christian church. This was a critical issue in Paul's conflict with the superapostles at Corinth. As we noted in the last chapter, Paul's own manner of speaking and presence in the community had become detrimental to his authority. Therefore, Paul was absolutely dependent upon the oral skill of the reader of his four-chapter letter to get the message of his letter across.

Sending an emissary to read a letter aloud was one of the most effective ways to establish one's apostolic presence in the early churches. Paul, like other ancient letter writers, was dependent upon trusted carriers to literally *deliver* their letters to recipients. Martin McGuire defines how important the letter carrier was to the writer in the first century: "The personal representative or messenger, the visitor or traveller, were almost the sole means of communication between nations and individuals."[19] Before sending the letter, the writer would "brief the carrier on the contents of the letters entrusted to them and also make supplementary reports on matters that were not set down in writing."[20]

Receiving a letter meant hearing both a message conveyed on behalf of the sender and a written document. Letters, therefore, bore a kinship with oral messages; like oral messages, the sender's name was placed in the beginning. The written document authenticated the messages. The carrier could also provide information about the writer of the letter. The letter, then, as written and conveyed, was one of the ways Paul overcame the separation from his churches. William Doty notes that "we gain a sense of the importance of his emissaries or letter carriers: they receive authority to convey the letters to expand upon them, and to continue Paul's work."[21]

Those who orally present Paul's letters to the church in our time have the same opportunity to continue Paul's work. Paul's emissaries were entrusted with a Word that was only minimally represented by the papyrus they carried. The kind of remote, detached and mechanical style of oral presentation that dominates in the worship experiences in today's churches would have been unthinkable to Paul. From his distance in time, Paul still challenges us to give voice to the authority and richness of the Word as expressed in his letters.

A study of our tradition of recitation informs us that we, as preachers, need to take more seriously the task of developing our own public reading skills and cultivate them in members of our community. The aim is to first become better listeners ourselves so that we can become better reciters and teachers of recitation. Listening and public reading are two ways of becoming equipped to preach in an oral-aural electronic age.

A THEOLOGY OF PERFORMANCE FOR LECTORS AND LISTENERS

Our effort to become better listeners and lectors in this electronic age depends on our developing a different theology of oral presentation. We must first redeem the concept of "performance." The idea that performance is associated with sham, pretense, or even sinful misrepresentation of reality has been shed in virtually every discipline of the social sciences. Performance studies is no longer the province of a trained elite of professionals in the dramatic or literary arts. Rather, metaphors of performance and theatricality are being used to describe not *imitation* but *creation* of social reality. To dramatize this expansion of interests, the Department of Interpretation at Northwestern University recently changed its name to the Department of Performance Studies to show how "the study of interpretation has . . . pushed beyond its traditional interest in printed imaginative literature to embrace the living oral traditions of real people."[22] This performative turn in the discipline changes perceptions of the importance of the reader in worship.

In the culture of silent print, the emphasis is upon the text as it appears printed on a page. To become effective, the reader examines the rhetorical features of texts such as word patterns and repetitions, parallelisms, alliterations, and the author's method of organization. Naturally, the reader places the text in a context to understand the sociopolitical and theological significance of the writing. Finally, the reader practices by reading the piece aloud, trying to convey with body and voice the literary conventions particular to the text. The process emphasizes the reader's role in serving the author's work and being the author's interpreter.

If one follows these guidelines, he or she will certainly become a better reader in worship. However, in an electronic culture, the emphasis shifts from text to speaker of the text. Audiences look for the speaker to engage them, to establish eye contact, and to convey the emotional values and states-of-being revealed by the text. As in the case of the early Christian communities, the lector in an electronic culture helps the community to understand itself and its reason for being. The lector performs text by embodying it, thereby returning it from the space of the printed page to the aural-visual space of the sanctuary.

As noted in the previous chapter, *performance* literally means "form coming through." Words printed and therefore fixed upon the space of a page are translated into the living oral and visual media of body and voice. Letters are read as conversations between writer and audience. Stories are told as stories. Psalms are spoken (or sung) as individual or corporate prayers uttered in community. Prophetic speech is declared with energy and conviction to the gathered listeners. Whatever the rhetorical form of a printed text, it "comes through" the lector. Performance of printed, silent texts restores the immediacy and dynamism of orality.

A performance of a text from Scripture is no less than an incarnation of that text, an event which creates and re-creates Christian community, and transforms all of the participants in the process—performer, text, and audience. The Presence that is sensed when reading the silent, printed Word becomes manifest in the performer's voice and body. Word takes on dimension in performance; no longer is it experienced in the interiority of the silent, private reader, but it becomes accessible to the entire community of listeners, who see as well as hear the performance.[23]

This is a call for reclaiming our rich heritage of recitation and for appropriating those insights in the way we present our sacred story in our time. It is not a call for developing a special class of individuals whose particular gifts and talents qualify them for the high honor of reciting texts in worship. When we tell jokes or personal stories in conversation, our bodies and voices become readily available to us and help us express ourselves. When we listen to a letter being read aloud, we can sense the author's presence in our midst. All of us know persons whose public prayers are nearly as evocative and eloquent as the Psalms. We can find ways of reciting these texts that suit us. There is a place for technique in improving our skill in this arena, but as Charles Bartow says:

Technique is not just a matter of getting control of the voice and body so that they obey the mind. Technique is itself an affair of the mind. Before it is a way of doing anything, it is a way of thinking, of being. Technique in speech communication is the way we put all that we are and can be into the service of content and purpose.[24]

We have no higher purpose than to become better listeners and better speakers of our sacred texts. They are the source of understanding our life together and alone before God, and their content is God's Good News.

EXERCISES

1. Work on becoming a better listener to literature. Attend a storytelling festival in your area and listen to these "texts" as they are returned to acoustical space. Make an effort to go to a community of faith different from your own and examine how the texts are rendered orally. What oral qualities are valued in this community? What do the texts sound like?

2. Set the following as a goal for yourself and for your preaching peer group: in the process of preparing your sermon, you will begin to speak your selected text aloud. After you have spoken it once or twice, make note of which parts of the text have resonance. Which words or phrases seem to stand out to you or to your group? Are there any other places you can remember where these words or phrases appear? The act of writing intensifies listening. Write an entry in your journal describing your experience of listening to the text. Imagine how the average person in your church would respond to an oral rendering of this text. What words or phrases would catch her ear?

3. After you have become familiar with speaking your text aloud in your sermon preparation process, turn your attention to the act of reading it aloud.

a. Type out your text on a piece of paper. Identify the words and phrases that carry the principle thoughts of the passage and mark them. Read the text aloud trying to emphasize the thought. Where are the transitions in themes or emphases in the passage? Work on pausing in these transitions.

b. Establish the phrasing of the passage.
Where do thoughts begin and end?

Are the sentences questions or statements?

Are they long or short?

Try reading the long sentences more rapidly than the short ones.

How does the rhythm of the passage convey the thought?

c. What are the emotional values of this text?

What is the state of mind of the author or narrator?

What attitudes are depicted among the characters?

Where is the tension in their relationship?

What is the author or narrator's relationship with the listener?

Work toward empathizing with these emotional values and conveying them in your reading.

4. Recite your text according to the form it is in. If it is a psalm, recite it as a prayer. If it is a letter, speak it that way. Whatever the genre, learn to speak it in that manner.

5. Learn to internalize all or part of a biblical story. Try to tell it to someone in your own words to get a feel for the plot. Work on retaining the structure of the story first, then begin to use the words as they are printed. Try to recite the story and retain 75 percent verbal accuracy. Work up to retaining entire narratives for reciting them in your congregation.

Chapter 6

The Listener as Active Participant

These listeners are my present concern, these who through old habit have already agreed in advance of hearing and therefore do not hear.

—Fred Craddock

Still be kind, and eke out our performance with our mind.

—Shakespeare

Michael A. King and Ronald Sider begin their excellent book on *Preaching About Life in a Threatening World:*

> We approach the pulpit, we preachers, with our frailties and our insecurities and our wistful hope that *this time* it will work, this time someone will care about what we have to say. In our dreams, the congregants lean forward, their eyes searching for new truth, their ears ready to take in any wisp of wisdom. In reality, a trace of expectancy quivers on the faces of the dwellers in the pews: just a trace. Once in a while full-fledged interest flares. More often, even that last trace winks out. Pews creak as bodies twist and slump their way down into comfort. What has gone wrong?[1]

What preacher has not shared this dreamy expectation of how a congregation might respond to "it," that is, a sermon-in-performance, only to know disappointment as listeners "slump their way down into comfort"? Sider and King have their fingers on the pulse of most preachers' performance anxiety. Preachers want to find ways to improve the quality of their oral presentations so that their congregations will get something out of the experience of listening to a sermon.

At the same time, they do not want to become merely entertaining in order to hold the congregation's attention. William Willimon fears

> that many preachers have capitulated to the "itching ears" of their congregations which desire to be entertained. They re-create the gospel in their own superficial image rather than allow the gospel to re-create them in its demanding image. Preaching arises not only out of the shape of the gospel but also out of the shape of the congregation.[2]

What is compelling is this author's reference to re-creation, images, and shapes in his discussion of preaching. The performance of a sermon is a process of being shaped by both sermon *and* audience. Performance studies offer an understanding of audiences as partners in the creation of what is said, done, and seen in the performance of texts. Audience members take the role of participants rather than passive observers.

This does not seem to be the spirit in which Willimon writes of audiences. Earlier in the same article he characterizes most audiences for preaching as "confused and lethargic" and unable to make much sense of the gospel unless it is explained to them "point by point." He criticizes those who, drawing from principles of narrative homiletics, preach "made-for-TV sermons" which cater to audiences of "people who want to be entertained rather than converted." The implication one draws from this article is that audiences do not *want* to work at making sense of what they listen to, so they favor some variation of "story-preaching," as if listening to stories makes listeners passive. What they need, suggests this writer, is a good, strong dose of exposition which "makes demands upon body and mind."[3]

Narrative *is* demanding. Narrative is a rhetorical form that creates a world where expectations are reversed and the order of things unsettled. This world is populated with characters, enigmatic strangers who make daring choices and puzzling pronouncements. In this "other" world there are different norms for behavior operating and seemingly insurmountable complications. Preachers who enter this terrain do so at their own risk, for narrative both reveals and conceals the selfhood of the preacher. The risk is as great for listeners. In order for the narrative to make sense, the listener must enter its world by investing both intellect and imagination. Listeners must remember, see, hear, taste, understand, make connections, ask questions, and even accept ambiguity and paradox.

Yet these qualities are precisely what make narrative such a desirable form for sermons. Narrators and listeners alike have a basic need to enter into other worlds and experiences in order to better understand the strangeness of their own worlds. To speak or listen to narrative is not to evade responsibility. On the contrary, narrative demands that we become more fully involved in our own world by examining our own stories. To demean or devalue this imaginative engagement is to misrepresent the form and function of this time-honored mode of speech.

Most writing about narrative or story in homiletical literature has emphasized the role of the preacher in making stories or narrative sermons come to life. What is usually missing is a complementary emphasis on the role of the listener in creating the sermon. Listening to a sermon-in-performance is neither consumption of an expository message nor is it "mere" entertainment. Good narrative is good exposition because it teaches as it delights.[4] Listening is work, play, and rigorous co-creation. To deepen your understanding of your role in speaking the sermon, you will need to deepen your awareness of what your listener's role is.

IMAGES OF AUDIENCE

Most of us have been influenced by models of communication that provide a very narrow perception of what the process of listening is. Communication theorist Paul Campbell puts the problem this way: "We have implied that the speaker or writer is the active agent, the one who persuades, while the hearer or reader is passive, the one persuaded."[5] In these models the speaker has all the power and the responsibility for persuasion. Which one of us has not had a speech teacher or consultant rightly emphasize the importance of the speaker's role in energizing a speech or oral presentation? But what images of the audience have you internalized while trying to understand your role as a speaker? The author of one textbook in particular goes even farther than Sider and King in casting the audience in a negative light:

> When you rise to make a speech, do not picture your audience as waiting with eager eyes and bated breath to catch your message. Picture it, instead, as definitely bored—and distinctly suspicious that you are going to make this situation worse. Picture your listeners as looking uneasily at their watches, stifling yawns and giving vent to a unanimous "HO HUM!"[6]

I, for one, am enervated by such a low view of the audience. I admit that imagining the audience as suspicious, skeptical adversaries might generate some energy to improve one's speaking skill. But how will you be able to continue to preach Good News week after week if you are feeding on negative perceptions of your audience? In a more recent textbook, speech consultant Sandy Linver gives a keener assessment of the listener's situation when forming an impression of a speaker:

> Every listener is asking the question "Why should I listen?" The question may be only subconscious, but it still is there, and you can't tell an audience to listen because it is good for them, at least not in so many words. No matter how much your audience needs your information . . . it is still your responsibility to hook them at the outset by signaling that what's to come will be stimulating and thought-provoking as well as informative. Coming on as pompous and pedantic, with a holier-than-thou attitude about what you have in store for them, will turn them off and create stiff resistance.[7]

These statements certainly ring true. Anyone who has ever faced an audience intuits that they have the power to make or break a speech. And we have all had those experiences of being in an audience in which the speaker was completely intimidated by his or her audience. Such speakers make frequent apologies about their presence or their subject, their strategy being that they will win our empathetic attention. We want those speakers to take charge, to accept their responsibility to make something out of this occasion, and involve us in listening.

On the other hand, we have also had experiences of listening to a speaker who assumed that all the power in the communication event belonged to him or her. Such speakers did not seem to notice or need the audience at all. All of the energy in the event seemed dependent on the skill and personality of the speaker. It did not really matter what the message was, or who the audience was, the speaker assumed that the power and authority for the message came from the personality and personhood of the speaker. What happens, though, is that a wide gulf of perception opens between the speaker and his or her audience. We do not tolerate a person who badgers us or talks *at* us in a conversation. Why should sitting in the pew be any different? Listeners do not pay attention to speakers who do not pay attention to them.

A PARABLE OF LISTENING

Recently I attended a church in a small town outside of a great city in the Southwest. I had attended the church with relatives a few years before and felt very much at home there. It was much like the church I had grown up in as a child. But this visit was different. All of the furniture had been removed from the chancel area. There was a single stand-up microphone in the center. Surprisingly, no one gave me a bulletin or any printed order of worship when I entered. The service began with singing but since there were no words before me I did not know how to participate. I felt anxious and disoriented because all of my "props" for responding had been taken from me. This had become an alien environment for listening. I did not know how to perform my role in worship. It was a bit like the dream one often has of being cast in a play and being expected to perform the role without knowing the lines.

The song leader led us through choruses that everybody else had memorized. No one used a hymn book and everyone looked directly at the song leader for direction. One song segued into another with the only breaks being when the song leader offered a brief homily about some aspect of living the Christian life. The piano and organ player played softly underneath these extemporaneous speeches. I made some notes about how like a television production this was shaping up to be. Stodgy, "churchy" furniture had been replaced with a new, spare setting. The instrumental backdrop for the song service was not Mr. or Mrs. Church Member on the piano and organ, but a highly sophisticated, prepackaged audiocassette tape, produced in a professional sound studio. The pace was tightly controlled, steady, and rushed. It seemed as if we were in some great hurry to get through the "preliminaries" and on to the preaching. It was as if the values of this part of worship were being shaped by those of electronic culture—speed, segue, efficiency, no pauses for silent reflection.

When the song service had ended, the pastor came up to the microphone. He spoke without notes and made free use of his body and voice. He frequently called for oral responses and sometimes asked for a show of hands of those who agreed with him on a certain point. He would occasionally refer to his Bible by holding it up but usually recited his references in a rapid-fire cadence. His eye contact was relentless.

In the article, I quoted earlier, Will Willimon worries that *forms* of preaching are unduly shaped by the values of electronic culture. He is concerned that preachers might take too many of their cues from "narrative homiletics" to fashion "made-for-TV" sermons. I would certainly agree that this preacher's *style* was suitable for television. He was dressed in cool colors; he was energetic, convicted, in control of his presentation, and exuded confidence, maybe even to the point of being *too* self-assured. He was definitely "on."

Yet the sermon itself was not narrative in any sense. It was, in fact, an *expository* treatment of a selected biblical text. This entire event seemed designed to overcome the perceived "confusion and lethargy" of a television-seduced audience by adopting the smooth, tightly organized style of the so-called electronic church. As a listener, I was certainly getting plenty of information about critical issues: sin, salvation, discipleship, eternity (and so on) in his careful, passionate, point-by-point exposition. I cannot speak for the other listeners on that occasion, but from my point of view, something else was lacking. There was no lack of personality, energy, and power in the style of the oral presentation of the preacher. And there was plenty of exposition and information about the gospel in the sermon. What I was missing was some consideration of the personality of the audience. Of the three components of a balanced presentation, speaker, message, and audience, awareness of the audience was the "something" that was lacking.

How can congregations be present as active listeners to the sermon if they are viewed as mere "passive-receptors" who do little more than consume messages delivered by "entertaining" preachers? As theater director Richard Schechner says: "The audience is not a . . . stagnant lump. Changes in an audience occur during performances as well as from one performance to another."[8] Transformation of self and audience by the proclaimed gospel is what Christian preaching is all about. The way audiences are present or absent in your process of creating and performing the sermon determines how they will be changed.

KEEPING THE LISTENERS BEFORE YOU

It was said of John Wesley that he would often sit in different pews and ask: "What would it be like to hear this sermon like 'John Smith'?"[9] As part of his preparation process, Wesley tried to listen as one of his listeners by actually sitting in the places where they sat, thinking the thoughts they would think, and thus create the language he would use in speaking his sermon. Those who have studied Wesley's preaching have wondered if the quality of his relationship with his listeners was the secret of his effectiveness as a speaker.

One of the mysteries of the Methodist movement was how John Wesley was able to hold the attention of a crowd whose idea of entertainment was going to a public hanging or bear baiting. The sermons that are printed in and of themselves do not explain Wesley's effectiveness. Bereft of stories or illustrations, they seem to have no "entertainment" value at all. Even his speaking style was reported to be "chaste, solemn, and conversational" in an era when other less famous preachers were highly expressive.[10]

Albert Outler, in his introduction to the first volume of John Wesley's *Sermons,* offers the following view of Wesley's preaching: ''After 1739 he was even more earnestly convinced that preaching, to be effective, must be an interpersonal encounter between the preacher and his hearers.''[11] A devoted student of rhetoric, Wesley chose not to adopt the highly favored ''ornate style'' of some exemplary English preachers such as John Donne. He also deplored the excesses of the Puritan preaching tradition in which

> the prophet-preacher's primary task was to find and expound a word from God to his hearers. . . . This in turn produced some intricate homiletical forms which, in lesser hands, tended toward the ponderous and pedantic ''crumbling of texts'' and to elaborations of heads and subheads.[12]

Instead, Wesley favored a ''plain style'' of speaking where simplicity and clarity were valued above all other homiletical virtues. In his *Directions Concerning Pronunciation and Gesture,* Wesley advises young preachers to ''endeavour to speak in public just as you do in common conversation. Attend to your subject and deliver it in the same manner as if you were talking of it to a friend.''

Part of this conviction came from Wesley's concern for those listeners who were marginalized in the society of his day. In his field preaching he wanted to break down the barriers created by class, education, and even organized religion. ''Wesley had found his new underclass where they were and had gathered them into new social groups in which each person found acceptance and a new sense of dignity. Whitefield and most of the other evangelists found their constituencies largely among the rising middle class and lesser nobility.''[13] As Wesley prepared his oral sermons, we can imagine that he kept before him even the ''common'' people who would gladly hear him.

A similar vision of audience appears in J.D. Salinger's novel *Franny and Zooey.* Franny, a young, intelligent college student, has just suffered a nervous breakdown while spending the weekend with her boyfriend. She has come home to recuperate and is badgered by her profane, cigar-chomping brother Zooey, who is a professional actor. Zooey is trying to understand why Franny is so convinced that reciting the Jesus Prayer offers any hope for the recovery of her spirit.

Then in a startling moment of self-recognition, Zooey remembers what his older brother Seymour once told him as he prepared to perform as a child on a popular quiz show. To meet little Zooey's objection that performing was meaningless because audiences were "full of morons," the brother instructs him to perform for "the Fat Lady." He does not explain who the Fat Lady is, but a clear image of her arose in little Zooey's imagination. The Fat Lady was the embodiment of all that was fearful, demeaning, ugly, and tedious about performance. The child imagined a figure who "sat on the porch all day, swatting flies, with her radio going full-blast from morning till night." Something about performing *for her* filled it with grace and meaning. Zooey tells his sister:

> I don't care where an actor acts. It can be in summer stock, it can be over a radio, it can be over television, it can be in a Broadway theatre, complete with the most fashionable, most well-fed, most sunburned-looking audience you can imagine. But I'll tell you a terrible secret—Are you listening to me? There isn't anyone out there who isn't Seymour's Fat Lady! And don't you know who that Fat Lady really is? Ah, buddy. Ah, buddy. It's Christ Himself. Christ Himself, buddy.[14]

John Wesley was one speaker who "knew the terrible secret" that Christ was present in, with, and as the audience. It was that Presence which helped Wesley learn to speak in ways common people could understand. Every preacher has an implicit theology of audience. Is Christ somehow present here or is the audience merely a "stagnant lump" with eyes and ears only for "entertainment"? Wesley deeply respected the capacity of his listeners to become full partners in his preaching ministry by keeping the image of conversing with them ever before him in developing his style. This image helped him make particular choices in his speaking. For example, in his instructions to young preachers, Wesley instructs them on some techniques for developing listener awareness:

> You should always be casting your eyes upon some or other of your auditors, and moving them from one side to the other, with an air of affection and regard: looking them decently in the face, one after another, as we do in familiar conversation. Your aspect should always be pleasant, and your looks direct.[15]

Wesley taught that the sound of the speaker's voice in the sermon should be as musical and variable in tone as it is in interpersonal conversation: "Nothing more grates the ear, than a voice still in the same key. . . . The best way to learn how to vary the voice is to observe common discourse. Take notice how you speak yourself in ordinary conversation, and how others speak on various occasions." He also believed that the "affections" of the listener could shape the ways the sermon "came through" the speaker's body.

> So that this silent language of your face and hands may move the affections of those that see and hear you, it must be well adjusted to the subject, as well as to the passion which you desire either to express or excite. It must likewise be free from all affectation, and such as appears to be the mere, natural result, both of the things you speak, and of the affection that moves you to speak them. And the whole is to be managed, that there may be nothing in all the dispositions and motions of your body, to offend the eyes of the spectators.

Perhaps the cornerstone of Wesley's effectiveness was preserving the congruity of heart-felt belief and the way one spoke to any listener:

> On all occasions let the thing you are to speak be deeply imprinted on your own heart: and when you are sensibly touch'd yourself, you will easily touch others, by adjusting your voice to every passion which you feel.

John Wesley looked to the dynamics of interpersonal interaction for clues to effective public speech. He understood that the speaker and listener shared the power and responsibility for communication. Preachers in all eras of the church who assume all the power for themselves are like one of Wallace Stevens's characters in "Notes for a Supreme Fiction." The poet writes of a Canon who, when speaking, "imposes orders as he thinks of them, As the fox and the snake do . . . But to impose is not to discover."[16]

What is there for a speaker to discover in the immediacy of direct and common conversations? Quite possibly the way "to enable hearers to walk down the corridors of their own minds, seeing anew old images hanging there, images that have served more powerfully than all concepts and generalizations in shaping them into the feeling, thinking, acting beings they are."[17]

Jesus told his audiences in Matthew 11:15: "Let anyone with ears listen!" Whether preachers like it or not, a listener is in fact listening to him or herself, that is, the whispering which arises from one's deepest interiority while listening to you. Preachers who do not understand this principle squelch the power of the listener to make meaning out of the sermon.

> For if the meaning of an utterance is based on the experiences of the utterer, there is the implication that the listener has no meaning of his own but somehow adopts the meaning of the utterer; and since meaning is . . . framed in language, there is the further implication that the listener must accept the language of the other, i.e., that as listener [she] has no language of [her] own.[18]

The devout Jews in the story of Pentecost, who were from every nation under heaven, were able to hear *in their own language* of the mighty acts of God. The Holy Spirit enables effective preachers to speak in an oral-visual language listeners can understand. If listeners are to be effective co-creators of sermons, they must be able to listen in their own language rather than simply be put in a position of accepting the language of "the other." That means displacing models of oral communication which cast the listener in passive-receptive roles with other models.

THE IMAGE OF THE AUDIENCE AS RECEPTOR

As our electronic culture began to develop, certain models of communication became dominant in speech textbooks. In 1949,

Claude Shannon and Warren Weaver published *The Mathematical Theory of Communication* in which they posited that communication begins with a "source" which formulates a "message," consisting of "signs" to be transmitted. A "transmitter" converts the message into a set of signals that are sent over a "channel" to a "receiver" which then converts the signals into a message.

Even though this theory was primarily concerned not with the *meaning* of messages but rather with their transmission, Shannon and Weaver's model became an analogue for communication in a variety of situations. The model helped explain the nature of television transmission to an audience who only then were beginning to be exposed to the media. Producers, directors, and announcers make up a "source." Air waves transmit the message to the receiver, which converts electromagnetic waves back into a visual impression for the viewer.[19]

Many textbooks extended this analogy into fields of human communication. The Shannon-Weaver model of communication, which was reprinted in one text after another, established the image of a speaker's brain as a source, the vocal system as the transmitter, and the oral and visual space between them as the channel. The message is received by the listener's ear and arrives at its destination, the listener's brain. Any distortion in the channel which masks the signal is called "noise."

The legacy of this model of communication appears in much of the descriptive language we still use to talk about speech. Speakers are often referred to as "senders" and audiences as "receivers," i.e., those who "get the message." Listening becomes a process of decoding signs and symbols which constitute the messages. Audiences are objectified into passive-receptive consumers of these messages that are sent by speakers. Listening becomes

> merely a "response" to or a "reception" of a message; and given such a definition of listening, one is committed to a definition of meaning as a property of the stimulus or a property placed in the message by the sender. The only function left for the responder or receiver is to decode or to react. In other words, the listener's role is to receive and respond to the message of another, to the meaning of another, indeed, to the language of another.[20]

When the activity of the listener is reduced in this way, it places a great burden upon the speaker to be the sole creator of meaning. While the Shannon-Weaver model of communication is no longer dominant in the field of human communication, images of audiences as "passive-receptors" still persist in our consciousness but do not fit our experiences as listeners.

THE PERFORMANCE WORLD OF YOUR LISTENER

Reflect for a moment on the listening habits of those who come hear you speak on Sunday morning. Some were awakened by the sound of a voice transmitted through a clock radio. A man shaved while he listened to news of a natural disaster in a remote part of the world where thousands of people died in an instant. A woman turned on a television set and was subsequently bombarded by ads for cars, vacations, and deodorants while she was dressing to come to church. Riding to Sunday school, a child caught a fleeting glimpse of a panhandler at a bus stop while listening to a favorite singer through personal headphones. When your listener arrives at church, he or she sits in a pew and tries to focus on the sound of your voice, your physical presence in the pulpit, and the linear sequence of your ideas. But while listening to you speak, the person may also be whispering to a spouse or friend, looking at the stained glass windows, or noticing the behavior of other listeners in the pews.

What makes it possible for any one of us to pay attention to so many things at once? It is, as Richard Schechner observes, the capacity to select what parts to pay attention to and what parts to absent oneself from. Without your ability as an audience member to practice selective inattention, you would not be able to listen to anything at all.

Think for a minute of your own behavior at, let's say, a folk festival. You are confronted with a wide array of performances in a particular area going on at the same time. It is not possible to give your full attention to each performance. You must make some choices of what you will pay attention to. On your way to hear a folk singer, you might stop to watch a magician or mime artist. You might decide to leave while one performance is going on in order to catch the beginning of another. No one seems to question or challenge the way your attention and inattention alternate.

I recently attended a conference-wide youth event in which participants staged a variety of events and performances at a church campsite. The purpose of the event was to raise money for various mission organizations sponsored by the area churches. I remember standing against a tree talking intensely with a colleague about some problem in ministry while a gospel music concert was going on all around us. Occasionally we would find ourselves "dropping out" of the conversation momentarily while some song was being sung or when we recognized a familiar performer. Very quickly, however, we'd "drop back into" the conversation as before. Even as I spoke to him, I watched a folk dance demonstration nearby. All the while, people we knew and did not know came and went, joined us for a while, and went away to some other site while eating and talking. My primary focus shifted from one performance site to another and back again many times during the event.

At no time did I feel that I or anyone else was *ignoring* what was taking place. On the contrary, I felt that I was very much involved with what was going on. It seemed certain that these social interactions were as much a part of this youth event as the aesthetics of music or dance. Greetings and conversations were as much a part of "watching" the performances as was bearing witness to the artistry of the performers. This personal experience bears out what Schechner observed at other events where directors incorporated the concept of selective inattention in their theatrical presentations:

> There was no necessity to maintain, or appear to maintain, a single-focus high-tension attention. But at the same time the use of selective inattention led not to a feeling of laxness or "I don't care," but to a selective discipline on the part of the audience.[21]

Audiences who come to church and who listen to you speak are living in a performance world where "spectators come and go, pay attention or don't, select what parts of the performance to follow. These habits may be further trained by television—because the ubiquitous sets are always turned on but often not looked at; or by the radio and phonograph which also encourage selective inattention.''[22] Whether they know it or not, church audiences are creating experiences for themselves in the "performance world" of the worship service.

At a recent gathering of a major denominational body, planners arranged a space where a group of volunteers would take turns reading the entire Bible through while the meeting was taking place in a great assembly hall. At any time, a spectator could enter the room, listen to a portion of the Scriptures being read aloud, and leave when he or she chose, knowing that she could return at any time during the meeting and listen again. Outside the room were other social gatherings of those who were attending or exiting the room. The comments and questions about the event among those *outside* added dimension to the experience of being *inside* while the event was going on. Some people came to spend a few minutes between sessions, listening to whatever passage was being recited. Others arranged their schedules so that they could hear particular parts of the Bible presented or listen to a particular reader. There were even times when readers found themselves reading aloud alone. Self became audience in a profound way.

At a recent festival of biblical storytelling, a group of biblical storytellers volunteered to take turns reciting the Gospel of Luke. Audience members were encouraged to come and go as their schedules permitted during the recitation. The recitation would take 4½ hours, the planners felt, and was to be divided into two sessions over two evenings. The storytellers understood that entrances and exits of spectators during the recitation was not a signal of rejection or refusal to participate, but was part of the rhythm of participation in listening. The performance was framed by prayer and singing, but during the recitation, some audience members left the performing space to make phone calls or to bring other family members (usually their children) to parts of the performance and then exit. Others would briefly cluster together in small groups outside the room while the recitation was going on. When a storyteller finished his or her piece, the teller would often step out of the room for a break, then return. To the surprise of the storytellers, most audience members stayed through the entire recitation both nights.

On each of these occasions, the responsibility of "attention" or "inattention" was shared with the audience. While some might initially have objected to the plan for these events as a serious violation of established conventions for "paying attention," they soon found that an entirely new form of engagement was taking place. This way of listening was more in keeping with the ways one listens or pays attention to the variety of performances which punctuate everyday life. As Schechner explains:

> As their attention "wanders" people begin picking up on events and images that would otherwise escape notice, or be merely blurred side visions: movements of spectators, gestures of performers not at the center of the scene, overall arrangement and dynamics of space. The performance can be contemplated; the spectator can choose to be in or out, moving her attention up and down a sliding scale of involvement. Selective inattention allows patterns of the whole to be visible, patterns that otherwise would be burned out of consciousness by a too intense concentration. . . . Through selective inattention spectators co-create the work with the performers. . . . In a real way the spectators become artists.[23]

There is much that is helpful in homiletical literature that stresses the art of the sermon. Preachers create sermons and then embody them in the act of performing them. Yet we have paid too little attention to the listeners' role in this art. For, finally, it is the listener who becomes an artist by making sense of what is spoken.

THE PERFORMANCE OF THE LISTENER

The sermon is a form of discourse that makes particular demands upon a listener. In order to "make sense" of the sermon, listeners do some very disciplined and hard work. Their creative work may take place in silent reflection or may be more active and take the form of acceptable oral response (such as "Amen!" or "Preach on!") "Paying attention" means keeping one's singular focus on the sermon as it is being performed.

Audiences may choose to pay attention or not, but they are certainly expected to sustain the meaning of the occasion by *appearing* to pay attention by their posture, body language, and level of conversation. It is unthinkable that people would breach conventions by talking out loud while the sermon is spoken or by walking around in the sanctuary. However, every preacher has some joke about an audience member who breaks these conventions at some point by falling asleep during the sermon or by being caught saying something in a pause during the sermon. There may be many who do not come to worship simply because they resist the particular conventions of listening that attend the preaching of sermons.

I remember sitting in terror when a particular evangelist would visit our church to preach a series of revival services. While his style of delivery was rather mild and conversational, he was known to interrupt his sermon to "call people down" who were talking or "acting up" during his presentation. If for no other reason, I paid attention because I dreaded the embarrassment I would suffer if he should talk to me that way! He demanded adherence to a strict code of audience behavior. Small wonder, then, that audience members are taught to conform to an image of themselves as "passive receptors" of an authoritative message delivered by a minister.

Performance theorists such as Paul Campbell and Richard Schechner have taught us that the center of effective communication has shifted. No longer is the center of meaning located between the speaker and the message (or between the actor and the script, the storyteller and the story, even between the preacher and the sermon) but is in the indissoluble unity between the speaker-message-audience. This means that, for the listener, meaning does not come from outside of the self, it comes from within. Listening to a sermon is not simply receiving the meaning transmitted in a preacher's message. Audiences cannot simply displace their own deeply internalized structures of meaning and adopt that of the preacher. Rather, they are either encouraged to or discouraged from listening to themselves in the performance of the sermon. The same process is at work when you read a book or watch a play. Arthur Koestler writes:

> The extent to which a character in a novel "lives" depends on the intensity of the reader's participatory ties with him. To know what

Hamlet feels while listening to the ghost, is the same thing as to know how it feels to be Hamlet. I must project part of myself into Hamlet, or Hamlet into myself . . . In order to love or hate something which exists only as a series of signs made with printer's ink, the reader must endow it with phantom life, an emanation from her conscious or unconscious self.[24]

As with any work of the imagination, the listener tries to find some way of projecting him or herself into the sermon you present. Since human beings have an irresistible need to enter other worlds, other selves, other experiences, we enjoy reading a novel, attending a play, or hearing a story. As audience members, we are given the opportunity to collaborate with the performers, to create the characters, settings, and images out of our selfhood. Interaction is the way we participate. "It is our own characters, our own enactments, that we listen to; we direct ourselves in the performance that we stage, in the roles that we take."[25] Like preaching, listening is also a performance in which projections come forth from the listener's most intimate self.

A sermon is not an object that stands outside of the space which is between preacher and congregation. It does not contain a secret message which is to be successfully extracted by passive-receptive listeners. It is, rather, an "inter/action." The prefix "inter" refers to place; the noun "action" names the experience of listening. When creating the sermon, the preacher can profit by taking on the role of the listener. Anticipating the performance of her sermon, the preacher asks:

1. What will this *sound* like to the one sitting here in this pew?

2. What do I look like from the perspective of the listener?

3. What other performances go on in the worship service that my sermon is an integral part of?

4. What other messages are conveyed in this sacred space which also command my listeners' attention?

5. What is my theology of audience?

In one sense, the site of the performance of the sermon is the pulpit. That is where the sermon comes through you, the preacher.

But in another sense, the site of the performance of the sermon is the space *between* you and the listener. It is there that the listener becomes co-creator of the sermon by:

1. imagining and thus creating the characters which populate the sermon;

2. imagining and thus establishing the settings for the action of the Gospel as proclaimed in the sermon; and

3. examining and incarnating the ideas present in the sermon by making them "present" in their consideration.

Listeners pay attention to your sermon by listening to themselves. Your sermon takes shape in their inner landscape even as it takes shape in your own body and voice. On that stage is where the power of the performed sermon is unleashed.

EXERCISES

1. Find a time when you can go into the sanctuary of your church. Sit in silence in one of the pews. This is where your listener listens to himself or herself when you speak. Pay attention to the space.

What is your eye drawn to?
How does sound carry in the room?
What does the pulpit look like from this vantage point?
What other objects in the space are invested with meaning?
What parts of the congregation's story begin to surface as you sit here?

Record your observations in a journal.

2. Put one of your own sermons on cassette tape. Then, if possible, listen to that tape on a personal stereo recorder while you sit in the sanctuary. What impressions do you receive as you listen to this sermon in this space?

3. Listen to a cassette recording of a preacher you admire. Visualize that speaker before an audience. What elements of this preacher's address show that he or she is aware of the audience?

4. If you are a part of a preaching peer group, try the following exercise: Begin speaking on a topic of your choice. It may be part of a sermon, it may be something entirely different. You must be prepared to speak without notes. As you speak, talk to each listener one by one. Speak to each one directly, as if you were in conversation. Work at reaching them with your eyes. After you have finished, ask your listeners to tell you if you were successful in "contacting" them. Ask them to tell you what improvements you can make to reach your listener better.[26]

Chapter 7

Arriving at the Joy of Preaching

I saw that there is nothing better than that
all should enjoy their work.
—Ecclesiastes 3:22

This book is about recovering the joy of preaching. It recognizes that the process of preparing and delivering sermons week after week can wear on the preacher and soon may tax his or her spiritual, emotional, and intellectual resources for proclaiming the Good News. Preaching usually arises out of necessity and is all too often a response to the blinding pain, gnawing grief, or even casual indifference brought to worship by your congregants. Yet the Gospel of Jesus Christ invites its preachers to consider the possibility that preaching can be joyful.

Joyful preaching is rooted in a deep satisfaction that comes from knowing who one is as a preacher, how one works and plays at it, and from trusting one's own voice and body to be available for the task. The Gospel we proclaim frees us to be authentic in the pulpit and to find new sources of energy for speaking the sermon.

Authentic preachers are those who embody the Gospel they proclaim in their manner of delivery. Hungry listeners respond to the preacher whose word is congruent with his or her presence in the pulpit, for that word then becomes incarnational. When a sermon is performed, that is, when the form of the sermon "comes through" the preacher's body and voice, listeners are transformed from passive recipients of message into active co-creators of meaning. Contemporary listeners are exposed to a bewildering array of mediated image and sound. A sermon can become the occasion when preacher, listener, and Holy Spirit create meaning out of the sounds and images evoked by the Gospel.

Unfortunately, too many preachers "act" like someone else in the pulpit. They carry borrowed behaviors with them when they speak and are often so enamored of "successful" preachers or dominant social characters that they attempt to imitate their style and manner of delivery. Imitative preaching is acting because the preacher is trying to be like someone else. What I have noted in this book is the difference between acting in the pulpit and working on the performance of the sermon. The performance of the sermon stresses that the end of the sermon is in the eye, ear, and experience of both preacher and listener.

In such a climate of noisy imitation as we have in our electronic culture, it is difficult to discover one's own natural voice for preaching. Images of success, crafted for television, radio, and print media, are in constant display in our mind's eye. We have, however, in the example of the Apostle Paul at Corinth, one Christian preacher who resisted the strong temptation to be like the media stars of his day. Grounded in his own interpretation of the Gospel, and empowered by his own personal story, Paul cultivated and presented an authentic voice of experience, thereby transforming the Corinthians' understanding of discipleship. His is the voice our tradition remembers, not those of the Corinthian superapostles.

The example of the Apostle Paul at Corinth teaches the contemporary preacher that cultivation and development of one's own voice for preaching is more than improving technique. It is easy to confuse matters of the heart with questions of style. The voice is the unique sound that comes from the recesses of one's own heart and soul. It is a sound that is shaped by one's experience of the Gospel in life and is revealed in the preacher's rhythm, pace, and vocal variation. Oftentimes discomfiting aspects of the preacher's self are revealed in the voice or in the action of the body. Anxiety, fear, self-doubt, pomposity, or arrogance appear as sound and movement. For example, glibness may sound like clipped and rapid speech, fear as garbled consonants or unfinished sentences, and self-doubt as a harsh overtone. Confusion or lack of a focus may look like wild gesticulation. Authentic preachers are those who face those dark parts of the self revealed in patterns of speech and bodily movement so that the Gospel can be released in and through them as they preach.

Careful attention to our own voices and bodies opens us up to the voices and images of biblical faith. Most of us have not been encouraged to *listen* to the biblical texts we speak upon each week. Nor have we been invited to imagine the worlds, the characters, and the events that are recorded there. We have become adept at extracting ideas or principles from them and explaining them in our sermons. Oral reading does not have to be a perfunctory rendering of a biblical text. It can be a *performance* of that biblical text in which sounds, images, characters, and language from other eras in Christian experience come through our own bodies and voices. Such experiential understanding of these sacred texts awakens both our imaginations and those of our listeners. The discipline of oral reading not only enlivens the task of reading texts aloud but also better prepares us to preach by giving us new angles of vision.

I began with a story of a child running joyfully down a hill. My hope is that you will experience a similar joy in preaching—that you have been energized to open up lost parts of your experience, to engage biblical texts with your senses, and to trust the sounds emanating from your heart. Speak well. Speak the truth. Speak from the heart.

Notes

CHAPTER 1

1. Paul Baker, *Integration of Abilities: Exercises for Creative Growth* (New Orleans: Anchorage Press, 1977), 17.

2. See chapters 9 and 10 in Clyde Fant's *Preaching for Today, rev. ed.* (San Francisco: Harper and Row, 1987).

CHAPTER 2

1. Orson Welles, *Moby Dick—Rehearsed: A Drama in Two Acts* (NY: Samuel French, 1965).

2. Lane Cooper, trans., *The Rhetoric of Aristotle* (Englewood Cliffs, NJ: Prentice-Hall, 1932), p. 8.

3. Ibid.

4. Sandy Linver, *SpeakEasy* (New York: Summit Books, 1978), 13-14.

5. Ibid., 22.

6. Robert Shaw, "Worship and the Arts." Whiteside Lecture, Cannon Chapel, Emory University, February 16, 1989.

7. Julien Green, *God's Fool: The Life and Times of Francis of Assisi,* trans. Peter Heinegg (London: Hodder and Stoughton, 1983), 137-38.

8. Paul Baker, *Integration of Abilities: Exercises for Creative Growth* (New Orleans: Anchorage Press, 1977), 38.

9. David Kelsey, "The Arts and Theological Conversation," *ARTS* 2:1 (Fall, 1989): 9.

10. Lillian Hellman, *Pentimento: A Book of Portraits* (Boston: Little, Brown and Company, 1973), 3.

11. Thomas Wolfe, *Of Time and the River: A Legend of Man's Hunger in His Youth* (New York: Charles Scribner and Sons, 1935), 22.

12. C. Hugh Holman quoting F. Scott Fitzgerald in the Introduction to *Of Time*

and the River: Young Faustus and Telemachus (New York: Charles Scribner's Sons, 1965), xiii.

13. Baker, Preface to *Integration of Abilities*.

14. Ibid.

15. Richard F. Ward, "The Sermon and Story: Creating the 'Other'," *Ministry and Mission* 15:1 (Fall, 1989): 3.

16. Robert Wilhelm, lecture, Storytelling Skills Institute, San Pedro Conference Center, Orlando, Florida, February 7, 1989.

17. Norman Friedman, *e.e. cummings: The Art of His Poetry* (Baltimore: Johns Hopkins Press, 1960), 83-84.

18. Ibid., 84.

19. Mircea Eliade, *Journal II, 1957-1969* (Chicago: University of Chicago Press, 1989), 70.

20. I am indebted to Dr. Clyde Fant of Stetson University for introducing me to these exercises.

21. Baker, Preface to *Integration of Abilities*.

CHAPTER 3

1. Lane Cooper, trans., *The Rhetoric of Aristotle* (Englewood Cliffs, N.J.: Prentice-Hall, 1932), 186.

2. Sandy Linver, *Speakeasy: How to Talk Your Way to the Top* (New York: Summit Books, 1978), 18.

3. Ibid., 23.

4. This is a thesis developed by Deiter Georgi in *The Opponents of Paul in Second Corinthians* (Philadelphia: Fortress, 1986).

5. Victor Paul Furnish, *II Corinthians* (Garden City, NY: Doubleday, 1984), 490.

6. Amos N. Wilder, *Early Christian Rhetoric: The Language of the Gospel* (Cambridge, Mass.: Harvard Univ. Press, 1964), 56.

7. At this writing, scholarship in performance history has not adequately focused on the participation of women in shaping ancient conventions of recitation.

8. Albert Lord, *The Singer of Tales* (Cambridge, Mass.: Harvard Univ. Press, 1960), 26.

9. Donald Hargis, "The Hellenic Rhapsode," *Quarterly Journal of Speech* 56 (1970): 388-94.

10. See Bruce Rosenberg, *The Art of the American Folk Preacher* (New York: Oxford, 1970): 6, 10.

11. Thomas Boomershine, *Story Journey: An Invitation to the Gospel as Storytelling* (Nashville: Abingdon, 1988): passim.

12. Thomas Boomershine, *Biblical Storytelling* (Unpublished manuscript), 1985:34.

13. Oscar Cullman, *Early Christian Worship* (London: SCM, 1953), 24, 30.

14. Eugene Bahn and Margaret L. Bahn, *A History of Oral Interpretation* (Minneapolis: Burgess, 1970), 30.

15. G.G. Ramsey, trans., *Juvenal and Persius*, Loeb Classical Library Edition (Cambridge: Harvard University Press, 1919), 3.

16. Pliny, *Letters*, 2 vols. William Melmouth, trans. (Cambridge: Harvard University Press, 1941), 5:371.

17. Pliny 9:34.

18. Ibid.

19. Bahn and Bahn, 39.

20. Victor Paul Furnish, The Anchor Bible *Second Corinthians* (Garden City: Doubleday, 1984), 490.

21. Robert Funk, *Language, Hermeneutic, and Word of God* (Evanston: Harper, 1966), 284.

22. Ibid., 223.

23. Ibid., 264.

24. Victor Turner, *From Ritual to Theatre: The Human Seriousness of Play* (New York: PAJ, 1982), 40.

25. Ibid., 110.

26. Tom F. Driver, *Patterns of Grace: Human Experience as Word of God* (San Francisco: Harper and Row, 1977), 122.

27. Ibid., 133.

28. Ibid., 134.

29. Ibid., 121.

30. Ibid., 130.

31. Ibid., 120.

32. Linver, 15.

33. Driver, 137.

CHAPTER 4

1. Paul Wilkes, "The Hands That Would Shape Our Souls," *Atlantic* 266:6 (December 1990): 88.

2. Book 1.2:9.

3. See George Kennedy, *Classical Rhetoric and Its Christian and Secular Tradition from Ancient to Modern Times* (Chapel Hill: University of North Carolina Press, 1980), 16ff.

4. Steve Sterner, Chapel Homily, Cannon Chapel, Emory University, April 16, 1991.

5. Eugene Lowry, "The Narrative Quality of Experience as a Bridge to Preaching" in *Journeys Toward Narrative Preaching,* Wayne Bradley Robinson, ed. (New York: Pilgrim Press, 1990), 67-68.

6. J.D. Salinger, *The Catcher in the Rye* (Boston: Little, Brown and Company, 1951), 131.

7. "A Poet's Advice to Students," *A Miscelleny Revised* p. 335

8. Suzanne Britt, "Aqua Velva Faith and Perma Press Certainty: Do the Calculated Effects of the Clergy Spring from Vanity or Hypocrisy—That Fatal Deception Signaling Death to the Spirit?" *Books and Review* 17:4 (Winter, 1990): 3.

9. *Persona* is a term used in a variety of ways in literature. I use it here to identify who you are when you speak the sermon.

10. Joseph Hough, Jr. and John Cobb, Jr., *Christian Identity and Theological Education* (Chico, CA: Scholars Press, 1985), 5, 15ff. Hough and Cobb build their notion of "characters" from Alisdair MacIntyre's *After Virtue* (Notre Dame, IN: University of Notre Dame Press, 1981), 26ff.

11. Hough and Cobb, 5 (n. 12)

12. Ibid., 78.

13. Ibid.

14. Jonas Barish, *The AntiTheatrical Prejudice* (Berkeley: University of California Press, 1981), 1-2.

15. Dwight Conquergood, "Communication as Performance: Dramaturgical Dimensions of Everyday Life" in *The Jensen Lectures: Contemporary Studies,* ed. John I. Sisco (Tampa: University of South Florida, 1982), 27.

16. I am indebted to Dwight Conquergood's explication of this definition from the *Oxford English Dictionary* in "Communication as Performance," 27.

17. Clyde Fant, *Preaching for Today,* Revised Edition (San Francisco: Harper and Row, 1987). See particularly chapter 10.

18. Don Wardlaw, "Using Video as a Resource for the Process" in *Learning Preaching: Understanding and Participating in the Process,* ed. Don M. Wardlaw (Lincoln, IL: The Lincoln Christian College and Seminary Press, 1989), 104.

19. Alla Bozarth-Campbell, *The Word's Body: An Incarnational Aesthetic of Interpretation* (Tuscaloosa: University of Alabama Press, 1979), 2.

20. Dietrich Bonhoeffer, "The Proclaimed Word" in *Theories of Preaching,* ed. Richard Lischer (Durham: Labyrinth Press, 1987), 29.

21. Phillips Brooks "The Two Elements in Preaching" in Theories of Preaching, ed. Richard Lischer (Durham: Labyrinth Press, 1987), 15.

22. Ibid., 17.

23. Linver, 43.

24. A "poem" for Bozarth-Campbell means *any* work of imaginative literature and is not a reference to a particular genre.

25. Alla Bozarth-Campbell, 2.

26. Ibid.

27. Ken Burns, "Television and History" in the *Atlanta Journal and Constitution* (March 13, 1991): A15.

28. See chapter 9, "Using Video as a Resource for the Process" in Wordlaw, *Learning Preaching: Understanding and Participating in the Process*, 157-200.

CHAPTER 5

1. Walter J. Ong, "A Dialectic of Aural and Objective Correlatives", *Critical Theory Since Plato,* Hazard Adams, ed. (New York: Harcourt, Brace, Jovanovich, 1971), 1159.

2. Walter J. Ong, *Orality and Literacy: The Technologizing of the Word* (New York: Methuen, 1982), 8.

3. Ong, "Dialectic," 1160.

4. "Born Again Christians Not Always Bible Readers," *Atlanta Journal and Constitution* (January 14, 1989) Section B, 14.

5. Mark Twain, *Tramp Abroad* Vol. 2.

6. S.S. Curry, *Vocal and Literary Interpretation of the Bible* (New York: Macmillan, 1903), 13.

7. Richard F. Ward, *Your Ministry of Reading Scripture Aloud* (Nashville: Discipleship Resources, 1989).

8. Ong, *Orality and Literacy,* 17.

9. Plutarch, *Life of Solon,* in *Lives,* trans. Bernadotte Perrin, Loeb Classics, I (London, 1914), 488-89.

10. Richard F. Ward, "A New Look at the Lector's Art," *Liturgy* 8:3 (Spring, 1990): 34.

11. Julian Hinton, *Performance* (London: Macmillan, 1987), 2.

12. Ong, *Orality and Literacy,* 3.

13. I am indebted to Dr. Thomas Boomershine for his adaptation of Walter Ong's "history of the Word" as found in *The Presence of the Word.*

14. Charlotte Lee, *Oral Reading of Scriptures* (Boston: Houghton Mifflin, 1974), 1.

15. Charles Bartow, *Effective Speech Communication in Leading Worship* (Nashville: Abingdon Press, 1988), 85.

16. Thomas Boomershine, *Biblical Storytelling* (unpublished manuscript, 1985), 47.

17. Oscar Cullman, *Early Christian Worship* (London: SCM, 1953): 24.

18. Boomershine, 45.

19. Martin McGuire, "Letters and Letter Carriers in Ancient Antiquity," *Classical World* 53.5-6 (1960): 148.

20. Ibid., 185.

21. William Doty, *Letters in Primitive Christianity* (Philadelphia: Fortress, 1973), 37.

22. Ibid., 46.

23. Ward, "A New Look at the Lector's Art," 36.

24. Bartow, 9.

CHAPTER 6

1. Michael King and Ronald Sider, *Preaching About Life in a Threatening World* (Philadelphia: Westminster Press, 1987), 9.

2. William Willimon, "Preaching: Entertainment or Exposition?" *Christian Century* 107:7 (February 28, 1990): 206.

3. Ibid., 204.

4. St. Augustine gives careful treatment of this rhetorical principle in Book 4 of *On Christian Doctrine.*

5. Paul N. Campbell, "Performance: The Pursuit of Folly," *Speech Teacher* 20 (1971): 268.

6. Richard C. Borden, *Public Speaking as Listeners Like It!* (New York: Harper and Row, 1935), 11.

7. Sandy Linver, *Speak and Get Results* (New York: Summit Books, 1983), 86.

8. Richard Schechner, *Performance Theory* (New York and London: Routledge, 1988), 193.

9. Robert Dolman, "Effects and Effectiveness of John Wesley's Preaching," Lecture, Cambridge University, August 5, 1989.

10. Ibid.

11. Outler: 14.

12. Ibid., 22.

13. Ibid., 17.

14. J.D. Salinger, *Franny and Zooey* (New York: Bantam Books, 1961), 200-202.

15. This and subsequent quotes are taken from John Wesley's pamphlet entitled *Directions Concerning Pronunciation and Gesture,* passim.

16. Wallace Stevens, *The Palm at the End of the Mind: Selected Poems and a Play,* Ed. Holly Stevens (New York: Vintage, 1972), 229-30.

17. Fred Craddock, *Overhearing the Gospel* (Nashville: Abingdon Press, 1978), 38.

18. Campbell, 268.

19. I am indebted to Stephen W. Littlejohn's discussion of this theory in *Theories of Human Communication, 2nd Edition.* (Belmont, CA: Wadsworth Publishing Company, 1983), 117-118.

20. Campbell, 268.

21. Schechner, 197.

22. Ibid., 206.

23. Ibid., 202.

24. Arthur Koestler, *The Act of Creation* (New York: Macmillan, 1964), 349.

25. Campbell, 271

26. This exercise is based on a similar one created by Speakeasy Inc. in Atlanta, Georgia, as part of their instructional program in speech communication.

ABINGDON PREACHER'S LIBRARY

Imagining a Sermon by Thomas H. Troeger
Imagination of the Heart by Paul Scott Wilson
How to Preach a Parable by Eugene L. Lowry
Designing the Sermon by James Earl Massey
Liberation Preaching by Justo L. Gonzalez